CONTENTS

INTRODUCTION

IRISH PEOPLE IDENTIFY THEMSELVES more with their counties than with any other place, apart from Ireland itself. The county is the core of local identity. Indeed, when the Government of Ireland Act of 1920 imposed partition on the island, the two new jurisdictions came to be widely known as 'The Twenty-Six Counties' for what is now the Irish Republic, and 'The Six Counties' for Northern Ireland.

The county has achieved this central place in popular consciousness for several reasons. Although the size of each one varies considerably, with the biggest, Cork, being about eight times larger than the smallest, Louth, nevertheless the counties are a relatively convenient size for identification purposes. The four provinces of Munster, Leinster, Connacht and Ulster are too large for people to relate intimately to them at local level. They retain certain uses, for sporting purposes, for instance, where inter-provincial competitions occur in Gaelic games and rugby. They also form a rough framework for elections to the European Parliament, although Munster is the only province whose borders correspond precisely to a European constituency. Leinster is divided into Dublin and Leinster outside Dublin, whereas Connacht and the three counties of Ulster within the Republic are lumped together as Connacht-Ulster. Northern Ireland, it is true, is often referred to as Ulster, but in this usage it assumes a state dimension rather than a local one. In general the provinces do not attract instinctive emotional identification in the same way as the counties.

At the other end of the scale, the lesser territorial units: baronies, parishes and townlands, are generally too small to be easily identifiable at a national level. The parish, in particular, did once play an important identification role for its members. But few outside the counties themselves will know the location of the parishes within them – hardly surprising, given that there are over 2000 parishes in the country. Everybody, or nearly everybody, on the other hand, knows the location of counties.

It is not surprising, then, that the instinctive answer of Irish people to the question, 'Where do you come from?', when talking to other Irish people, is to give their county. The questioner in turn will usually hasten to assert whatever connection they may have with the county themselves, maybe even going as far back as their grandparents. The county, therefore, features quite frequently in Irish discourse, as a means both of geographical and, to some extent, of social and cultural identity, both at home and abroad.

Indeed, the experience of emigrants was a powerful factor in heightening a sense of county consciousness at a popular level, at least since the huge exodus during and immediately after the Great Famine of 1845–50. At that stage many emigrants were still more likely to identify themselves first and foremost with the parish – some perhaps with the even smaller unit of the townland – than with the county. But as they came to be flung together in the electoral wards of New York or Boston, neither the townland, nor even the parish, provided a sufficiently broad base on which to establish circles of collaboration, of mutual support, of trust. County identities then came to subsume more local ones. People from the same county tended to cluster in particular areas. On the lower east side of Manhattan, where today Chinatown and Little Italy jostle for space, there were areas specifically identified as 'Cork' or 'Kerry' wards as early as the 1850s.

County associations began to be established in New York from the 1840s, indicating that it

IRELAND
County by County

INTRODUCTION BY J.J. LEE
CONTRIBUTORS: DAMIEN ENRIGHT, IAN HILL,
CORMAC MacCONNELL, SEAMUS MARTIN

PUBLISHED BY
SALAMANDER BOOKS LIMITED
LONDON

A Salamander Book

Published by Salamander Books Ltd
8 Blenheim Court, Brewery Road
London N7 9NT
United Kingdom

ISBN 1 84065 157 1

A CIP catalogue is available for this book from the British Library.

All correspondence concerning the content of this volume should be addressed to Salamander Books Ltd.

CREDITS

Editor: Alice Duke
Designer: John Heritage
Copy Editor: Dorothy Mitchell Smith
Captions: Alice Duke
Picture Research: Alice Duke
Map: Janos Marffy (© Salamander Books Ltd)
Typeset: SX DTP Ltd, England
Colour reproduction: HBM Print Ltd, Singapore

9 8 7 6 5 4 3 2

Printed in Spain

Note: Although Belfast is a city within the county of Antrim rather than a county in its own right, the authors and publishers felt that its importance as a political, cultural and economic centre, merited its inclusion as a separate chapter.

INTRODUCTION

Professor Joe Lee is Head of the Department of History at University College, Cork. A member of the Royal Irish Academy, he has been an Eisenhower Fellow in the USA, where he has also held several visiting professorships, including a Chair of Irish Studies at New York University. His book *Ireland 1912–1985: Politics and Society* was awarded the Donnelly Prize at the American Conference for Irish Studies as well as an Aer Lingus/*Irish Times* prize for literature.

CONTRIBUTING AUTHORS

Damien Enright spent 32 years living in 'exotic places' before returning to his beloved Munster from where he has written for several national newspapers, including a weekly column for *The Examiner*. Also a published poet, his work has appeared in the prestigious *Poetry Ireland Review*.

Ian Hill is a regular contributor to the arts and travel pages of national broadsheet newspapers on both sides of the Irish Sea and is a frequent broadcaster on the BBC. He has written and edited numerous travel books, many of them concerning Ireland.

Cormac MacConnell worked in Dublin as a journalist for the *Irish Press* for many years before eventually deciding to follow his heart and move to the calm and tranquility of the province of Connacht. From here his colorful, if unorthodox, descriptions of daily life are frequently sought by newspaper and magazine editors in Dublin and abroad.

Seamus Martin is a staff journalist with the *Irish Times* in which capacity he has covered a number of major world events, including the transition to democracy in South Africa. He was also Moscow correspondent for that newspaper from the last days of the Soviet Union until the re-election of Boris Yeltsin as president in the summer of 1996.

CONTRIBUTING PHOTOGRAPHERS

Colman Doyle (Connacht) began his training under the famed photographer Norman Ashe, before joining the *Irish Press* group of newspapers where he has worked for more than 40 years. He has been voted Irish Photographer of the Year no less than seven times.

Tom Kelly (Leinster) started life as a freelance photographer in 1975 since when he has travelled extensively throughout the Third World. He is currently based in Ireland and has recently completed two successful photographic books on the Irish landscape.

Richard Mills (Munster) won his first photography award in 1967 when he was voted University College, Cork Photographer of the Year. Since then his spectacular images of Irish wildlife have been widely published and repeatedly acclaimed. In 1989 he was Highly Commended in the BBC Wildlife Photographer of the Year competition.

Geray Sweeney (Ulster) has worked as a very successful freelance photographer in both London and Belfast for over 15 years. She has exhibited her work several times in both cities and is currently living and working in Belfast.

Half-title page photograph: A holy well on Mary's Island, County Wexford.

was the county that featured as the unit of identity for the immigrants. They held meetings, dinners, balls, and outings, which in some cases continue to the present day. Photographs of these gatherings provide as good a clue as any to the rising social aspirations of the men and women of Irish-America, their affluence obviously increasing over the years. County associations were likewise founded in London, in particular, as emigrants to Britain grouped together, whether for defensive purposes, for psychological reassurance, for social networking, or just for nostalgia.

The county, then, came to acquire a more central place in popular consciousness as the 19th century progressed. It had, it is true, existed for several centuries. Thanks to the important pioneering work of Kenneth Nicholls of the History Department of University College, Cork, we are now able to confidently trace the history of the counties in medieval and Tudor times. The Anglo-Norman conquerors were the first to begin establishing them, immediately after their invasion in the late 12th century. By the end of the 13th century most of the country had been divided into counties, often bearing the names still used today. But their boundaries were generally very different, tending to be based on the pre-existing boundaries of Gaelic lordships. As the Norman colony declined in the 14th and 15th centuries, many of the counties disappeared, or their borders shrank until the original ones were often forgotten. It wasn't until the Tudor conquest in the 16th century that the county system in its modern form came to be established. Although the borders of a number of the present counties have been slightly changed since then, our county system is still essentially an inheritance from Tudor times, now about four centuries old.

But there was no reason for most people to identify themselves with the county until the 19th century. It was only very gradually, for instance, that even the middle classes, much less the lower orders, got the vote, or became familiar with parliamentary politics. As constituencies came to be based mainly on the county, and as more people came to be involved in the electoral process, the county achieved an important role in political terms. Constituencies today do not necessarily follow county lines. Several counties are divided into more than one constituency. But if counties are too big to form a single constituency, then it is still sub-units of the county which form the constituency, like Kerry North and Kerry South, or Galway East and Galway West, with the county name claiming precedence. If, on the other hand, they are too small, they are then joined with another county, as in Carlow-Kilkenny, Longford-Roscommon, Cavan-Monaghan, or Sligo-Leitrim. This joining together causes considerable unease in any county which loses its independent electoral existence, and the voting patterns can often vary greatly according to the county identity within the constituency. Outside the city areas, there is no constituency in the Republic which doesn't contain a county name.

The county, then, is a key building block in parliamentary representation. It is also a key unit in local government, since the Local Government Act of 1898 established county councils. It is true that local government is emasculated in today's Ireland, which is a highly centralised country – by some criteria the most centralized in Europe. Although local government is kept in a vice-like grip by central government, nevertheless there are regular local elections, and local politics revolve, outside the main urban areas, around the county. Politicians with aspirations to play a role at a national level normally deem it indispensable to establish themselves at a county level first.

Politics, administration and migration enhanced county consciousness in the 19th century. So did improved communications in general, especially with the coming of the railway and the telegraph in the middle of the century. Growing literacy in the second half of the century created a market for more newspapers, which often took county names, like *The Kilkenny People*, *The Clare Champion*, *The Wicklow People*, *The Tipperary Star*, *The Roscommon Herald*, *The Kerryman*, *The Derry Journal*, etc. While these reported news from further afield, nevertheless they cemented the place of the county as the main unit of social reference for their readers.

But it was probably through sport, and particularly Gaelic sport, that the county achieved its highest profile in the popular mind. The Gaelic Athletic Association (GAA), which was established in 1884 to promote specifically Irish games, soon came to enjoy quite astonishing success. Despite a turbulent early period, with the Association being torn by internal conflict among different types of nationalists, the sports went from strength to strength. The games of hurling and Gaelic football attracted huge crowds. The All-Ireland Championships became the most eagerly supported of all sporting endeavours in the country. In the early years, it was the club team that won the County Championship that participated in the national contests. But they did so as county representatives. Soon the county team came to be selected from the best individual players throughout the county, irrespective of their club, and thus became genuinely representative of the county as a whole. While it is not unknown for a player from one county to play for another county, it still happens only very rarely.

Nothing rouses county fervour more than the success of the team in the All-Ireland Hurling or Football Championship. When traditionally successful counties experience a barren spell, many a conversation turns to the crisis in county fortunes. Emotions ran high in Tipperary, for instance, the birthplace of the GAA, and a leading hurling county, when eighteen years passed after 1971 without the ultimate prize. There was a corresponding outpouring of pride and joy when the barren spell ended in 1989. In 1995, Clare enjoyed an even more emotional triumph, winning their first 'All-Ireland' since 1914, and in 1996 Wexford crowned a memorable hurling championship by recapturing the glories of earlier years with another famous victory. The emergence of Offaly in the 1980s as a hurling force greatly enhanced the profile of the county. In football, particular significance was attached to the first 'All-Ireland' triumphs of Down, Donegal and Derry (two of them of course from within Northern Ireland), late comers to the taste of victory, but all the sweeter for that.

It is difficult to convey the cluster of emotions that find expression in the elation of victory, or the depression of defeat, in Croke Park on All-Ireland Day. Indeed, as other bonds of community weaken in an age of gradual atomisation under media pressure, sport, and above all Gaelic sport, provides the single most significant bonding element in sustaining county identity.

Although Tudor county boundaries are now more than four centuries old in many cases, they have shown remarkable staying power. County boundaries, it is true, are sometimes breached for administrative purposes, with counties, or bits of counties, lumped together into more rational, or allegedly more rational, administrative units, in the shape of health boards, planning regions, tourism boards, etc. Nevertheless the county retains sufficient administrative functions, as well as historic and sporting associations, to ensure that it will remain at the centre of the Irish sense of place as long as such a sense survives.

All the counties have acquired personalities of their own, and retain distinctive associations, even for those who have left them to follow their fortune at home or abroad. They have attracted in their own right substantial literatures in prose and poetry, in ballad and song, which add depth and dimension to those personalities. Several have acquired proud or affectionate nicknames, a sure sign of a place in the popular heart, like 'the rebel county' for Cork, 'the banner county' for Clare, 'the royal county' for Meath, and 'the wee county' for Louth. The county colours have become a synonym for the county itself – the green and gold of Kerry, the red jersey of Cork, the black and amber of Kilkenny, the sky blue of Dublin, and the lily-white of Kildare.

Evoking county identities is not as simple as it may seem. Some of them are as elusive and intangible as they are real. No doubt many readers of this pioneering volume will think of something else they would wish to have included. But inspiring that wish is itself one of the objectives of the enterprise. And every reader will learn much from these surveys, as the authors guide us gently along their favourite county pathways.

PROFESSOR J. J. LEE
HEAD OF THE DEPARTMENT OF HISTORY, UNIVERSITY COLLEGE, CORK

THE PROVINCE OF
MUNSTER

MUNSTER IS THE LARGEST province in Ireland. It is a rich and confident province, having three of the Republic's six cities, four of her great rivers, and the great flow and estuary of the Shannon, longest river in Britain and Ireland. It has a massive diversity of landscape, from the most fertile, the Golden Vale, to the least fertile, the naked limestone plains of north Clare. There, in the Burren, it has the greatest polarity of botany, where indigenous flowers found elsewhere only in the Alps and Mediterranean lowlands grow side by side. It is at the northernmost range of Lusitanian vegetation, and Kerry and Cork have fuchsia hedges, rhododendron forests, and plants found nowhere else north of Spain.

Of all the provinces, it has the longest Gulf Stream coast and the mildest climate. It may rain, deep in the west, but there are a greater number of frost-free days here than anywhere north of the Channel Isles. Migrant birds flock in their hundred thousands to Munster estuaries in winter, and Cape Clear is the oldest bird observatory in the Republic.

The Munster coast is the native holidaymakers' favourite, and who would know better than the Irish themselves? Of Ireland's 66 Blue Flag beaches (those meeting European Union standards relating to water quality and general cleanliness), 26 are in Munster. For the saltwater fisherman, it is lapped by the most fertile sea – three-quarters of all specimen sea fish are caught in southwestern waters. Here, the first sharks of summer are hooked, tagged and released, drifting north on the Gulf Stream. Whales pass by, and giant leather-back turtles circumnavigating the Atlantic from their nesting beaches in the Caribbean. For the inland angler, Munster rivers hold the most bountiful stocks of brown trout, and almost every river has a respectable salmon run. Waterville is one of the best sea-trout lakes in Europe.

Kerry also has a very large colony of natterjack toads which live in the

Left: A music shop in Kenmare, County Kerry. The Kerry fiddle style, like so many other strains of traditional Irish music, enjoys worldwide popularity.

Above: The Common Darter is the most widespread dragonfly in Ireland. It is known to have migratory habits and can be seen in the southwest of Ireland sometimes as late as mid-October, up to a month later than other dragonflies.

dunes backing the five-mile (8 km) long strand at Inch. The elegant snow white egret, a new visitor, favours the southwest and if it nests in Ireland, as is the birders' hope, it is likely to be in Munster. Munster has, also, a richer variety of warm-blooded wild creatures than any other province, being the main redoubt of the pine marten, bank vole and red squirrel. The Munster people are warm blooded themselves, and famous for sport and song.

Munster was the nursery of many a journeyman saint who set out from stone cells by lake and sea to carry the Christian light to Dark Age Europe. The oldest surviving Christian church in Ireland is Gallarus Oratory, near Slea Head, and the first Protestant church built in Ireland is in Bandon, County Cork. Everywhere the landscape is dotted with relics of an earlier worship: stone circles and dolmens, their capstones like altars under the vault of the sky.

Munster has always produced Irish patriots and liberators. It was Brian Boru, from Clare, High King of Ireland, who defeated the Vikings. The ancient abbey that tops the Rock of Cashel-of-the-Kings rises dramatic and lovely out of the Tipperary plain. Daniel O'Connell, 'the Liberator', was born in Kerry; Michael Collins, who led the fight for Irish independence in 1919–1921, was born and died in west Cork. The cottage in which De Valera, our first *Taoiseach*, was reared was at Bruree in the Golden Vale.

Cashel is only one of thousands of ruins of old Ireland still extant in Munster. Cork has 2000 prehistoric sites, and Limerick's Lough Gur offers fine examples of early lake dwellings. County Limerick, alone, has 400 castles. Everywhere in Munster one comes upon elegant, roofless abbeys; squat oratories; ivy-bound churches; gutted stately houses.

It is also quite likely that Munster was home to the first potatoes, imported from America and welcomed at Youghal by Sir Walter Raleigh, also an import to Ireland, but not so welcome himself. At Youghal, also, was possibly smoked the first pipe of the insidious tobacco – but we can blame Raleigh for that.

Munster has some of the finest progenitors and practitioners of Irish music among the people of Clare. Ireland's composer, Wallace, of Waterford, was Munster born, as was the modern composer, Sean O'Riada, and the great poet in Gaelic, Aodhagán O'Rathaille. In science, Munstermen also made their mark – Boyle, of Boyle's Law, was born at Lismore Castle in 1627.

For sporting, the Munster people are famous. Jack Doyles, the boxer, was born at Cobh on the Shannon Estuary. Cork also has more All Ireland Hurling medals than any other county, and was home to the legendary hurler, Christy Ring. Its road bowlers sling a bowl with greater flair and accuracy than any others, lobbing hedges and curving corners, champions of Ireland again and again.

Munster vies with Leinster for fame in horseflesh. The first steeplechase ever was galloped between the steeples of Buttevant and Doneraile, in County Cork. The fine stud farms of Tipperary and north Cork are famous everywhere. Sons of Shergar, prince of stallions, can be seen grazing the parklands on long, slim legs. Vincent O'Brien, doyen of trainers, has his stables, still in business, at Ballydoyle.

Master MacGrath, the world-beating greyhound, was pupped in Waterford. Munster offers the finest, most scenic golf in Europe, with four world-class links courses close together in Kerry and Clare. The oldest yacht club in the world is on Cork harbour.

Being the most beautiful, Munster is the most filmed province. *Moby Dick* was made off the Cork coast; *Ryan's Daughter*, on the coast of

Kerry. Craftsmen abound, and the finest crystal glass in the world, often imitated but never equalled, is made in Waterford.

In Munster, the softest Irish and the most melodious English is spoken. When Cork men or Kerry women speak, you might think they were singing to you. This is, perhaps, one reason why visitors fall in love with Munster.

The old Irish Tourist Board slogan claimed, 'The most interesting people come to Ireland . . .' Many come to Munster, and they stay. There is hardly a village along the southwest seaboard that isn't host to a well-known expatriate writer, painter or film-maker and stars of stage, screen and pop choose Munster to bring 'quality' and privacy into their lives. These glitterati are welcomed, but in no way do they eclipse the light of local talent. Humour is the breath of life and the tradition of talk, song, dance and banter is treasured. Native vernacular brilliance blossoms behind every bush.

Below: Skellig Michael, one of the two Skellig Rocks which rise, gaunt and romantic, out of the Atlantic off the coast of Kerry. These beehive huts, which still cling to the clifftop 700 feet (213 m) above the sea, were built in the 6th century by members of a religious order whose successors remained on the island, cut off from the world by eight miles (13 km) of often raging ocean, for the next 600 years.

CLARE

County of stone and song

THE AWESOME Cliffs of Moher in north Clare rise 700 feet (213 m) out of the sea like black ramparts. Great slabs of paving stone, etched with the fossil tracks of creatures of a million years ago, wall off the more dangerous corners along the cliff path. The bare cliffs wear a toupee of green fields, across which the wind blows. It blows towards the Burren where there are no fields at all.

Someone once told Cromwell that the Burren was a 'savage land, yielding neither water enough to drown a man, nor a tree to hang him, nor soil enough to bury him . . .' Cromwell, being interested in doing all these things to the Irish, didn't bother to go there.

However, the description is hardly accurate. There are no trees, but scoops in the limestone plains support dense thickets of hazel and scrub. In spring, the 116 sq miles (300 sq km) of Burren stone is a wild rock garden, colonized by a disparate and wonderful botany. Blue Spring Gentians, Cinquefoil and plants rare or absent elsewhere in Ireland grow in profusion. Mountain Avens, found in the high Alps, bloom side-by-side with orchids normally confined to the Mediterranean.

It is a surprise, almost a shock, to come upon the Burren landscape. It is hard to believe one is still in Ireland, indeed hard to believe one is on earth, for the miles of flat, naked rock, stretching as far as the eye can see, are more reminiscent of our image of the moon. The low, bleached hills, also of limestone, might be outcrops in the Sahara, more so when seen through the staggering air of a hot summer's day.

These grey plains, or pavements – and pavements they are, with deep fissures between – were made from the compressed skeletons of plants and animals which, 340 million years ago, died on the floor of a warm, carboniferous sea. Limestone easily erodes, and the cracks are the result of water running over the pavement and finding their way underground.

Left: Bloody Cranesbill is the most spectacular of the eight varieties of geranium that are found on the Burren.

Right: Water from an underground stream trickles over the limestone scree of the Burren. Joined to the surface by potholes, some as much as 100 feet (30m) deep, the subterranean geography of this strange place is a maze of winding waterways and caves; Pollnagollum, 'the cave of pigeons', runs for eight miles (13 km) below the earth.

Above: No less than 23 native species of orchid are found on the Burren, none of which has been artificially introduced, including this very distinctive Bee Orchid.

On green oases, small farms dot the landscape. A red barn may appear in one's carefully framed photo of a dolmen, with washing in the yard on a line. Sheep graze the fields, eating, perhaps, rare Alpine flora. One imagines that at least a few of these weird plants have taken the opportunity to escape to richer pasture.

Here, stone forts, wedge graves and dolmens are much more common than farms. Man settled on the Burren 10,000 years ago and from his visible remains one might think that in Neolithic times the place was a veritable metropolis. In fact this was not the case. It is simply that the stones have been left undisturbed, there being no land to plough around them, and no need to use them for building. Loose stones are plentiful on the Burren.

Poulnabrone is one of the more accessible, and famous, of the table stones. It has featured on Irish postage stamps. One can stand beneath the canopy stone and, should the rain clouds pass over, it would make an adequate shelter from the weather. It is set on a slight mound, stark and dramatic against the sky.

Deep within Ailwee Cave, which is on the edge of the Burren, it is so dark that one's eyes could never become accustomed, however long one stayed. Long gone are the Irish bears that once slept there in winter. Cave bones have also included those of African wildcats, reindeer and Arctic foxes, animals as disparate in habitat as today's plants. We, ourselves, probably made homes in these caves not so very long ago in the scale of time. Stalagmites, no thicker or longer than a pencil, rise from the cave floor. Many commenced growing before the birth of Christ.

Holy wells are everywhere in the Burren, each patronized for its particular cure. Thus, the waters of St Senan's Well in Kilshanny were held to cure blindness, while sufferers from backache went to the well at Killnaboy. St Brigid's Well, a cure for all ills, is still a place of pilgrimage on Garland Sunday, at the end of July.

At Corcomroe are the ruins of a great abbey, open to the sky. At Kilfenora, a sleepy town on the pavement's edge, are found three High Crosses and the remains of a fourth, their Burren stone carved with intricate detail.

Perhaps it was the wind over the limestone pavements of the Burren, or the waves breaking on the treeless coast that inspired the airs of Clare, but whatever the cause, the county has nurtured the very soul of Irish traditional music, from the piping of Willie Clancy to the lilting ballads of Christy Moore. Each year at Lisdoonvarna, the capital of the Burren, a summer musical festival draws folk singers and musicians from all over the world.

As well as being a musical centre, Lisdoonvarna is also a mecca for lonely bachelors. Each September, following an old tradition, unmarried farmers from all over Munster leave their cows, and spinsters their spinning wheels, to come to the town in search of life partners. For a whole month, match-makers ply their ancient trade while their clients dance, drink and make eyes at one another. By the time they leave, some will have sealed a bond. Others, not having found their fancy, will wait for another crop, another year.

Above: Daniel O'Connell, who led the mass Catholic political movement of the early 19th century, won his first parliamentary seat in Clare in 1828.

Below: A county of music, the airs of Clare are played all over Ireland.

Right: One of four portal dolmens to be found on the Burren, Poulnabrone, which dates from between 2500 BC and 2000 BC, is certainly one of Ireland's most dramatic monuments. The large tilted capstone was raised by a system of levering. Some of these capstones are huge: at Brownshill Dolmen in Carlow the capstone weighs over 100 tonnes. This trapezoidal capstone at Poulnabrone measures 12 x 7 feet (365 x 213 cm). The name Poulnabrone comes from poul na *meaning 'hole of' and* brone *meaning 'quern' or 'milling stone' and so translates as 'hole of the milling stone'.*

110,589.

CORK

'On the banks of my own lovely Lee'

Cork is ireland's biggest county. It stretches from the rich lands of the Golden Vale in the north, to the flat lands of the east, to the Poor Law peninsulas and mountains of the west. To the south is the sea.

Long ago, it was the hub of Neolithic settlement and worship. The county boasts more stone circles per acre than anywhere in these islands, more than 2000 prehistoric sites, littered, as casually as furze bushes, over the landscape. Look behind a bush and you may find an undiscovered dolmen. The more notable sites, like Drombeg, are advertised; it would require a forest of finger-posts to announce them all.

Cork, the county capital, is a sleepy city, one that – compared with Galway, Limerick or Kilkenny – hasn't woken out of the Edwardian era. But with the Shandon bells ringing out over it, the Lee flowing through it, and high hills rising from its riverside streets, it is a more romantic city than most.

It is famous for 'de paper', the *Cork Examiner*, now gone national and dropped the 'Cork'. 'Cork' is a name of mixed blessings, translated from *Corcaigh*, 'a marsh', on which the city was built. When the notorious Black and Tans and British Auxiliaries burned Cork city in 1920 during the War of Independence, they went west looking for trouble with burnt corks in their hats.

East County Cork is noted for Ballycotton, a small fishing port, which, along with Ballymacoda, is a great estuary for wintering birds. Youghal, where tradition has it that Sir Walter Raleigh planted the first 'spud' and smoked the first cigarette, is an old walled sea port. It is a popular summer resort for the Irish, with a hurdy-gurdy amusement park and funfair still there 40 years after my childhood visits – Perks Amusements, it is called.

Cork north of the River Blackwater is the Golden Vale of rich

Left: Once an illegal sport in Ireland, bowling has remained a game of the rural back roads which were traditionally chosen for their terrain and privacy.

grasslands, cheese, butter and fat farmers. Here, Edmund Spenser, of *Faerie Queen* fame, had vast lands at Kilcolman, whence the gentle poet preached repression of the Irish so bloody that even Elizabeth I's colonizing government would not entertain it.

If Dubliners think of Cork city as the 'sticks', they consider west Cork as an arcane island on the southern seaboard. With the exception of Galway's Connemara, no other county has a region so distinct and a people so distinctive that it is given its own name. 'North Cork' refers to geography; 'west Cork' stands for a culture. It is a culture much sought after by 'blow-ins'. Coast and hinterland are speckled with the renovated cottages and mansions of famous writers, film-makers and artists. However, the 'native' culture remains thick on the ground.

Much of west Cork is a hilly land of small, colourful fields, with lichen-grown rocks that look like they have had orange paint splashed on them. Washed by the warm Gulf Stream, it is, in popular perception, the exotic land of rhododendron, fuchsia hedges, and picture postcard islands upon which peacocks roam. As one goes west from the city, the coastal strip of rocky land, with breaks of gorse and heather, becomes wider. Forty miles (64 km) from Cork, it stretches on both sides of the road, south to the sea and west to the Kerry mountains.

The west Cork people are no less colourful and individual than their landscape. It was here, during the war for Irish independence, that Flying Columns practised their daring guerilla tactics. Michael Collins, the ill-fated leader who signed the 1921 Treaty with Britain, was born in west Cork and shot there by other Irishmen, at *Beal na mBlath*, 'the mouth of the flowers'. Today, west Cork people are still proud and independent, a

Above: Cork harbour is a popular site for grey heron during the winter months when their numbers swell from 4000 resident pairs to between 9000 and 12,000 birds.

Right: Emigrants leaving the port of Cobh in the 1940s. Situated on the Cork Estuary, within hailing distance of Cork city, this pretty cathedral town was the last port of call for many thousands of Irishmen and women who decided to seek their fortunes in the New World. For most this was probably the last glimpse of their homeland they would ever have.

nation unto themselves, crowing at one another in sing-song voices, imaginative, rebellious and out of date.

The agricultural citizenry of Cork are fierce followers of sport, none more so than the west Cork farmers. Sulky racing and road bowling are favourites. 'Sulkies' are game little horses that pull a light cart and driver around a track which may be a stretch of country road, or a beach with the tide out. It is unforgettable to watch horses and drivers raise spray from the near pools or race far off in a string against the sun-bright Atlantic. It is intoxicating to hear the cries of the punters, the galloping commentary on the tannoy. Here is racing in the vernacular: sulky and saddle racing; county men and women riding flat out across the sun-blessed Irish sands.

As a state of mind, west Cork may well be retreating west. Twenty miles (32 km) from the city, the up-market, yachting town of Kinsale – 'gourmet capital of Ireland' – bears little resemblance to, say, wild west Dunmanway or Skibbereen. In Dunmanway, on market day, one sees battered cars and tractors, men in caps with rolled down Wellington boots, and sheep in the back of Toyotas. This kind of exotica has long since disappeared from Kinsale.

The division is also economic. The farmer of the rugged hills and coast is a grizzled, hard-working heir to Poor Law land, a turf cutter, fisherman and all-round dealer, keeping his family on 50 acres (20 ha), 20 of them arable, the rest rock and bog. But, they say: 'When God made time, he made plenty of it.' So, he finds leisure time for beagling – pronounced 'bagel-ing' – with hounds that rarely catch a fox, sulky racing, road bowling and hurling. He does not shave on weekdays, and has a drink at weekends, driving the tractor to the pub.

West, in the Irish-speaking area of Ballyvourney, on the rocky farms of Hungry Hill or Roaring Water Bay, we are a long way from the huge, rich fields of the Bandon Valley and Barryroe where the milk quotas are high, the new bungalows have central heating, and the farmers sport four-wheel-drive jeeps. Yet, there is an affinity among the people. The landscape may be drained and tamed, but let no stranger say that the people are any less 'west Cork'.

Above: The Golden Vale is a rich expanse of pastureland which covers north Cork, Limerick and most of Tipperary. It is reputed to be one of the most concentrated dairying areas in Western Europe.

Right: The mute swan (Cygnus olor) is found throughout Ireland. There is a resident population of about 10,000 with a particularly fine herd at 'the Lough' in Cork city. The word 'swan' is very old and derives from that for 'non vocal sound' – probably a reference to the wing beat – and the mute swans are known to make a lovely musical sound with their wings as they fly. They are 'mute' in comparison with the whooper swans (Cygnus cygnus) which honk constantly. About 8000 whoopers migrate to Ireland from Iceland during the winter months; they are shy birds but can often be seen in the string of reservoirs and adjoining fields of the Lee Valley, west of Cork city.

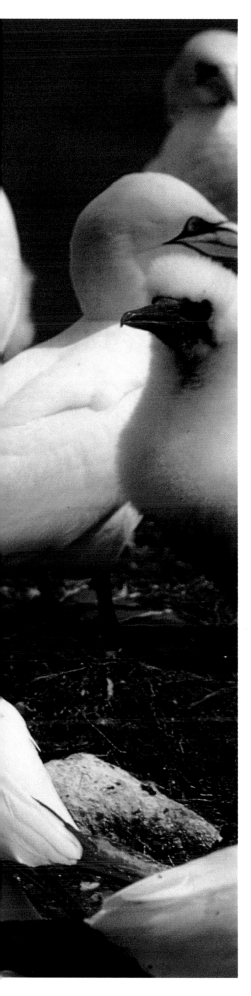

KERRY

Little climate, but much weather

THE KERRY PEOPLE are held, by the rest of the Irish, to be 'cute', not in the American sense of being pretty – although, of course they are that – but in the sense of being able to outsmart their fellow countrymen at every turn.

They are also, out of jealousy, the butt of jokes, such as, 'Did you hear the one about the Kerrymen who decided to climb the mountain? The scaffolding collapsed at 500 feet . . .' Kerry people are also known for their ability to answer a question with a question – this is part of their 'cuteness'. Asked if there is any chance of catching a few fish in his local wide stretch of the Atlantic Ocean, the dyed-in-the-bog Kerry person will eye one cutely and respond, 'Is it the way you're fond of fish?'

Everything in Kerry is superlative. In Sneem, there is 'the best selection of woollens in Ireland'. Near Waterville, a bar claims 'the most famous view in Ireland'. Caherdaniel boasts 'the only beach bar in Ireland'. On a lonely bog road to the Skelligs, a guest house cum wine bar suddenly appears offering 'the best Chinese and Indian food in Ireland'. In self-confidence, the kingdom is next door to Texas.

Whatever the hyperbole, the physical beauty of Kerry is world class. It can indeed claim elements of greatness. If a Greek friend told me about Ephesus or an American friend about Big Sur, I would take them to the Ring of Kerry.

In summertime, the landscape of the Iveragh Peninsula is splashed with colour. There is scarcely a square foot of grass that is not speckled with wild flowers; each small field a jewel in 'the Ring'. Heather purples the road side; fuchsia reddens the paths; montbretia edges the verges; loosestrife brightens the bogs. The rock faces are painted with contrasting grey and yellow lichens. Above, the clouds, moving across the sun, pattern the hills.

Left: The island of Little Skellig off the coast of Kerry provides nesting sites for 22,000 pairs of gannets, making it the second largest gannetry in Europe.

Kerry is a county with little climate, but much weather. The warm waters of the Gulf Stream wash between the open fingers of land. Temperatures are rarely less than 5°C (41°F) in winter, or more than 20°C (68°F) in summer. But, for all that, the main constant for much of the year is change. Mists or rain clouds drift in like veils off the western ocean. The sun, bright a few moments before, shines between them like a spotlight sweeping over the hills. 'Softness' is the theme, and water, a pellucid, magical light.

The misty lakes and grandiose mountains were the epitome of the scenery celebrated by the romantic movement led by Sir Walter Scott. When Queen Victoria visited them, she was smitten instantly. Although familiar with the loveliness of the Scottish Highlands, she pronounced the Kerry panoramas the finest in her Empire.

Turf cutting is big in Kerry. The drying black stooks of turf stand in the summer bogs among the yellow flag irises, the white bog cotton and the deep and bronze pools. To strip the bogs is a pity. They sit like brown, hump-backed animals in the mix of landscape. It takes a million years to make a bog and its unique flora, once gone, is irreplaceable.

Kerry is known for the romance of its islands, the Blaskets and the Skellig Rocks. The Blaskets, hard berths for man or beast, are thrown out into the Atlantic, off Dingle, the last land in Europe. Until the 1930s they were home to a mere 30 souls, including one Tomás Ó Crohan, whose

book, *The Islandman*, is a testament to the faith and stoicism of a simple man and his island neighbours. When measles and whooping cough came to the island, he wrote, 'Three months I spent sitting up with those of my children who took them worst, and I got nothing for the time I spent, only the two best of them were carried off. That was another discouragement for us, God help us. I fancy the sorrow of it never left the mother, and from that time she began to fail, for she was not to live long, and never lasted to be old.'

But, if there was tragedy on the island, there was also great joy and humour, and a great spirit in the people. He speaks of selling lobsters to a passing vessel in a rare time of plenty, 'It was a good life in those days. Shillings came on shillings' heels . . .' He tells of the bonanza of cut timber swept off the deck of a ship; of his childhood; his first visit to the mainland. He writes of match-making and wedding feasts; of gathering seaweed; of seal hunting. He brings to life the love and faith of these unique folk. 'We are poor, simple people, living from hand to mouth. We were apt and willing to live, without repining, the life the Blessed Master made for us, often ploughing the sea with only our hope in God to bring us through. We had characters of our own, each different from the other, and all different from the landsmen. I have done my best to set down the character of the people about me so that some record of us might live after us, for the likes of us will never be again.'

Left above: A rose chafer clings to hogweed on the Dingle Peninsula in County Kerry. This species is found mainly in the southern half of Ireland where it tends to have a very localized distribution.

Left below: The last 22 inhabitants of Great Blasket, the largest of the Blasket Islands, were finally evacuated to the mainland in 1953. With no longer a school nor a doctor on the island, the dwindling population – mostly bachelors – had become increasingly isolated.

Below: Portmagee on the Iveragh Peninsula by the Ring of Kerry which stretches from Killarney for nearly 40 miles.

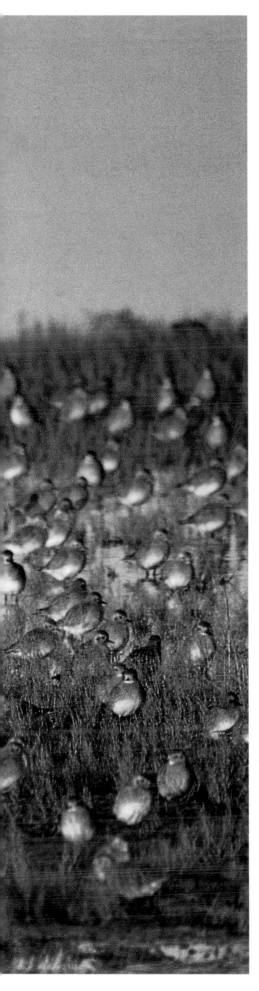

LIMERICK

A deceptive county

LIMERICK PEOPLE will tell you that Limerick women are the prettiest in Ireland. They point to the pages of the Irish *Tatler*, and photos of pretty girls at race meetings. Almost invariably, they are Limerick girls they say. However, to insist that they are beautiful above all other women in Ireland is extravagant. Women in every county are pretty, although this was not always the case. In the 1950s, farmers daughters tended, more than they do today, to plaster over their natural beauty with make-up and black mascara.

The natural outdoor looks of Irish women have since become fashionable, and the soft Irish climate is good for the skin. Irish women are extremely confident and 'well able' for the men. They are not short of words, or wit, or character. In ancient Ireland, they were total equals, and Brehon Law absolutely upheld their right to divorce a husband on the important grounds that he was weak in bed.

Limerick women, much prized, are like their county, neatly manicured. In Limerick, one does not find the wild disarray of Kerry, Clare or west Cork. Fields by the road side are flat and lush, with the finest growth of grass in Ireland along the Golden Vale. Here, happily, in early summer, old meadows still sway with the heads of tall and diverse seed grasses, dock, dandelion, clover and plantain.

The roads through the back country are mainly straight. As we drove, the world about was entirely pastoral and gentle, the villages few and far between, the cottages by the roadside small and built before the age of shoebox bungalows. On a mound heaved out of the plain, a square keep, with the ruin of a tall gable, once a Norman fortress, broke the skyline.

At Bruff and indeed at crossroad pubs all that Saturday afternoon, we saw cars parked, small boys in suits and little girls playing in their First Communion white dresses, pretty veils and bouquets askew. A few

Left: A flock of golden plovers create a spectacle on the mudflats of the Shannon Estuary, a haven for thousands of migratory birds during the winter.

Above: It is traditional in Ireland for friends and relations to award a child a generous gratuity upon taking their First Communion. Even after an initial splash on crisps and Coca Cola, newly Confirmed minors are likely to find themselves richer by half the average weekly wage.

carried little white purses, no doubt crammed with their communion gifts of £5 and £10 notes.

Everywhere is lovely in May in Ireland, but for those who enjoy wilderness, as embodied in the wildness of migrant birds, the Limerick shore of the Shannon Estuary is most spectacular in the winter. The Shannon, the longest river in Britain and Ireland, daily deposits a rich icing of silt in which billions of humble invertebrates breed, providing fat fare for the many birds that fly extraordinary distances to winter there. Knots breed 2000 miles (3218 km) away, in the thin tundra of the high Canadian Arctic; tiny dunlin, after breeding, fly south from Iceland. From Greenland, white-fronted geese wing in to Shannon. The great river obligingly recedes twice daily, exposing thousands of acres of invertebrate rich-mud.

The survival of the estuary is vital to the survival of its indigents which Ireland has an international obligation to conserve. No less than six species of birds are present in internationally important numbers. They are as much natives of Ireland as anywhere and spend half the year here. They may be born north of the Arctic Circle, but which comes first, the goose or the egg?

Out on the marshes of the Shannon, one realizes that Limerick is a deceptive county. The great estates and sylvan softness of the grasslands might be a thousand miles away. Limerick has been well-settled for millennia; Stone Age forts, castles, keeps, churches and modern towns abound. But the shores of the vast Shannon confluence are as wild as anywhere in Ireland. They are especially magnificent on a winter evening when the mudflats are gilded by the dying sun.

On the low islands, a thousand lapwing stand facing into the wind, their topknots dancing. Between them, dunlin skitter like clockwork mice. On the creeks, rafts of teal and widgeon drift in the evening silence, heads under wings.

Every now and then, as if by some unknown telepathy, all the waders rise together. Lapwing lift and wheel, black and white wings chequered against the sky. Above them, great flocks of golden plover soar and circle. Curlew beat into the wind. Then they all descend, light as feathers.

My favourite moment is when dunlin come. At breathtaking speed, they flash and bank in formation over the roosting flocks. You can see this wildness any winter evening on the Shannon marshes. Just a short distance from Limerick city, but it is timeless. It is glorious. It is free.

Above: The Shannon Estuary is one of the most important wintering sites for lapwing, attracting up to 30,000 birds, often many more in a harsh winter.

Left: The complexions of the Irish were historically differentiated into two types: the Fionn Gall, *'fair foreigners', and the* Dubh Gall, *'dark foreigners'. The* Fionn Gall *had creamy skin, freckles and red hair, while the* Dubh Gall *had white skin, raven hair and blue eyes. Of course, there are many variations in Ireland today, but one still encounters outstanding examples of both.*

TIPPERARY

Hunters and hurlers

TIPPERARY IS A RICH inland county with a town called Golden and mountains called the Silvermines. Approaching from the south, mountains edge the Tipperary plain on both sides of the main Cork to Dublin road, made more dramatic by snow in winter and blazing gorse in summer.

The great plain of Tipperary has many impressive raised bogs, one of the best known being the Littleton Bog. Here, pollens from the peats and mosses that have grown and decayed in the bog over the last 12,000 years provide geologists with an very accurate record of the vegetation, climate and agriculture of a geological period which has since become known as the 'Littletonian' era.

The history and ruins of time abound in Tipperary. One of the most magnificent of ancient Irish relics is the Rock of Cashel-of-the-Kings which emerges out of the Tipperary plain like something out of a medieval fairytale, an Irish Avalon. Seen from afar, it epitomises the legendary grandeur of early Christian Ireland and the power of the Irish Kings. It is even more impressive close to.

Tipperary is the only county in Ireland with a North Riding and a South Riding. The term 'riding' was first used in Domesday Book to define an administrative district. Ireland did not have William the Conqueror's census-takers, but all the same 'riding' is a division very appropriate to a county associated with horse flesh and horsemanship. Hunting is the sport of Tipperary's landowners. Hurling is the vernacular sport, and is followed with a passion. Tipperary horses and hurlers are some of the greatest that have ever graced a field.

The county is full of Norman names: Delaney, Delahunty, D'Arcy – the one-time hunters – now mixed with the old Irish names: the Ryans, Mahers, Dwyers, and so on. So many Ryans are there that they often

Left: Originally bred by William Barton in 1807, the Tipperary foxhounds are today one of Ireland's most prestigious hunting packs.

Right: The sheer power of the puck and the velocity of a well-hit sliothar *is awesome. It burns through the air, well beyond the speed of the eye. Local junior and senior hurling matches can be seen almost anywhere in Munster on a summer evening or Sunday afternoon and to watch any match, not just between the famous teams from Cork, Tipperary or Limerick, is a spectacle not to be missed.*

Above: Brian Boru, the formidable Irish ruler, whose victory over the Danes at Clontarf in 1014 ensured him a place in the national pantheon, was crowned King of Munster at Cashel in 977 AD.

enjoy local distinction in an agnomen. I remember, as a child in Thurles, being told that my friends, whose surnames were Ryan-Bishop and Ryan-Bucket, came from two different branches of the family and therefore 'lived on different sides of the tracks'. Whether this was literally true, I'm not sure, but certainly the main Cork to Dublin railway line, which crosses Tipperary and neighbouring Kilkenny, still runs through Thurles.

Both counties are hurling mad. When the 'Tipp' team was in competition, flags would be hung out of windows and the towns bedecked in the county colours. The same applies today. When driving along the Cork to Dublin road, the visitor will notice that on crossing the border into County Kilkenny, trees, lampposts, overhead wires and suspended teddy bears, hitherto dressed in the blue and gold of Tipperary, abruptly convert to the black and amber of Kilkenny.

Hurling is one of the fastest, fiercest games ever devised. It is played on an oversized football pitch, and the small leather ball, seamed with ridges, is almost constantly in the air as it is pucked or run from one end of the field to the other. The hurley sticks – or *camáns* – are hip high blades of ash, slimmer than hockey sticks, with broad bosses often bound with metal hoops.

Unlike a hockey stick, a hurley stick may be swung at any height, and the famous 'clash of the ash' occurs when two or more hurlers leap for the descending ball, their *camáns* colliding against the sky. It is a miracle – and a testament to the skill of the hurlers – that no player is decapitated, or suffers the full force swing of the instrument across the face. Nowadays, some hurlers wear helmets, but it is a recent innovation and not favoured by many experienced players who would rather trust the opposition not to harm them than suffer the discomfort of a helmet during the 70-minute long, sweaty game.

Hurling is – with the possible exception of steeplechasing – the most exciting sport in Ireland. The score tallies are high and smacking the ball over the high posts from 70 yards (64 m) out is a favourite scoring ploy. This is not easy while running full pelt, hopping the ball on the boss – it is against the rules to 'hand' the ball for long – and dodging the gauntlet of swinging sticks wielded by the opposition. It requires a cool head and deadly accuracy to score – look up for a second, toss the ball high, aim, swing and let fly.

Southern Tipperary is hunting country. While some hunters may hurl, and some hurlers hunt, average citizens can more easily afford a hurley than a horse. If they follow the hunt, it is likely they will use the traditional transport of Shanks's mare.

At the other end of the scale, the 'sons' of the legendary stallion, Shergar, still walk tall across the south Tipperary grasslands. The Derby winner, spirited away in 1983 in a failed ransom bid, is still mourned and his bones are sought like relics. His bloodline is perpetuated in Tipperary stud farms and his progeny remain much prized by horse breeders all over the world.

Coolmore Stud is one of the most important bloodstock breeding stations in the world, with associate farms in the USA and Australia. Flat race and National Hunt mares are brought here, where 40 to 50 stallions provide service. Open to the public, the best time to visit is undoubtedly in the early morning when the horses tend to be standing knee high in mist, their nostrils issuing fine smoke into the Tipperary dawn.

Below: The Rock of Cashel was the seat of the kings of Munster from about 370 AD until 1101. When St Patrick visited it in 450, King Aenghus is said to have allowed himself to be baptized, an undertaking which apparently involved being stabbed through the foot with Patrick's crozier, and is said to have left the newly Christened king lame for life. The Rock was finally granted to the Church in 1101 by King Murtagh O'Brien.

WATERFORD

Ireland's best kept secret

WATERFORD DEFIES GRAVITY. While other Irish counties boast of statues that move and windowpanes that reflect the Virgin Mary, in only one will a car run uphill when one releases the handbrake. The phenomenon can be relished at Waterford's Mahon Falls.

The people of Ireland rightly believe there are more things in heaven and on earth than our philosophers have ever dreamed of. Leprechauns are an endangered species, but the paranormal is still extant. Happily, *pishoges,* or supernatural valedictions, remain potent forces, protecting duns, raths and standing stones from the incursions of drainers, developers and European Union grants. It was intelligent of their builders to attach such warnings, and the curses pertaining to their removal, unwritten but passed down locally over thousands of years, are as old and durable as the artefacts themselves.

Waterford is a 'sleeper' among Irish counties, as beautiful in its way as any, but largely ignored and unknown. The Waterford people are private and laid back, and haven't pursued tourists with the same vigour as commercial Kerrymen or 'quaint-ifying' Galway city burghers. Used to employment on the great estates, with which the county is replete, they were satiated or stultified beyond bothering. It is extraordinary, for instance, that in the lovely town of Lismore there was hardly a 'Bed and Breakfast' available until five years ago, and one still can't buy a meal after six o'clock.

Waterford is a 'corridor' county. Folk disembark from the UK ferry at Rosslare, in Wexford, and rush through Waterford en route to Killarney, as if the latter were Mecca and there was nothing but desert in between. This, apparently, bothers the Waterford people not a whit. They don't mind keeping their beautiful inland mountains and stunning seaside strands a secret. Far be it from them to tout for custom. Let the visitors

Left: Built by King John in the 13th century and later acquired by Sir Walter Raleigh, Lismore Castle is currently owned by the Duke of Devonshire.

shoot through to Killarney, only alighting for the briefest of moments.

It is a source of amazement to many native Irish that tourists bother to go anywhere at all. It is almost certain, anywhere in our fair country, that unimagined beauty is only a short walk away and, in any case, to understand Ireland and feel that much-sought lack of stress and hurry, one is better staying put.

With a little patience, inner peace is reached: a herd of cows strolls at evening through the village; in the morning the children can be heard singing their tables in the National School; the church bells ring for the Angelus in a street where there isn't a cricket stirring, and at night the village pubs are filled with a buzz transcending worldy cares. Yet, nightly in B&Bs, visitors survey their maps: Kinsale tomorrow; Killarney and the Ring next day; Connemara the day after and 'we'll do' the lakes of Leitrim before a mad dash cross-country to catch the boat home. Such insanity defeats the object of the exercise, and nowhere is this more evident than in the tourist's gallop across Waterford, one of the loveliest, most tranquil counties in Ireland's crown.

The city of Waterford, famous for its crystal glass, was a Viking port, the name honouring Odin's father. Captured by Strongbow, the Norman invader, in 1170, it uniquely proved too strong for Cromwell in 1649. His 'by Hook or by Crooke' threat referred to seige routes via Hook Head or Crooke village on the estuary. In the event, he had to eat his words. The city's medieval walls are better preserved than any in Ireland, except Derry, and the townscape and quays are a wonderful sight from the Kilkenny side of the River Suir.

Below: Although subsistence dairy farming had existed in Ireland for about 300 years, it wasn't until the turn of the century, when Waterford became home to Ireland's first milk processing factory, that dairy production in the area underwent a period of rapid development. Today, Waterford represents one of Ireland's principal milk producing regions.

Dungarvan is the county town, with a large square, without a statue, little changed from what it might have been in the 1940s or 1950s – one can imagine asses and carts tied to the lampposts as farmers did their business on market day. Down a short street behind it lie the docks, where is evidenced that symbol of recent Irish 'quaint-ifying', a large building with exposed and re-pointed stone. As usual, the sandstone blocks of which it is built are coloured from deep red to umber, and it emulates a mini-Canary Wharf in London, only it is old and real. Here, too, are a few colourful pubs, outside which one can sit in clement weather and watch the yachts in the basin.

On a positively continental sweep of the Cork road above Dungarvan town, the motorist will be arrested by a magnificent view in his rear mirror; he should pull into a lay-by and get out. Below him, or her, will be seen the vast panorama of Dungarvan Bay, with bird-friendly wetlands and mudflats reflecting the sky. The itinerants camped nearby enjoy one of the finest views in Ireland, and their piebald ponies a fine diet as they graze the 'long acre' – the county name for lush, roadside verges – rich with a diversity of flowering weeds and grass.

Ardmore, on the coast, is distinguished by a ruined cathedral, not very large, but with a fine, pencil-slim round tower rising above it. This tower is one of the best examples in Ireland. The door is 12 feet (3.7 m) up the wall, the better to pre-empt Viking brigands and house-breakers, although the assailants were, as often, Christian Irish chieftains who saw no reason why monks should be richer than themselves.

The tower is still almost as perfect as when it was built. Swallows flit in and out of the windows and make it their snug home. Here is one place where their nesting sites are unlikely to be threatened, and for centuries generations of Lismore swallows have returned annually from Africa with every chance of breeding success.

In the cemetery beneath, Catholic and Protestant names are mixed, as is often the case in Irish churchyards. In the suntrap of the roofless old cathedral, two ogham stones, carved with ancient runic characters, stand propped against the wall.

From Ardmore, a road may be found to take one north to the River Blackwater on the verdant banks of which, at Lismore, vast King John's Castle stands. This venerable heap is not actually so ancient. There was a castle there, built in 1185, but later destroyed by Cromwell. However, the present edifice is nothing if not imposing with its castellated battlements and towers rising over the river, surrounded by the tall, exotic trees of the lovely Lismore estate. The view from the bridge below is one of classical tranquillity, the big river approaching on a straight course and then meandering off between lush watermeadows.

Above Lismore are the Knockmealdown mountains, heavily forested with great stands of mature deciduous trees and later tall lodgepole pines. After passing a corrie lake near the top one comes to the Vee, and here the traveller is rewarded with one of the most breathtaking views in Ireland. The blanket bog below gives way to a great, green plain, the Galtee mountains to the left; Slievenamon 'mountain of the women' straight ahead; the Comeraghs close by and, in the distance, the Silvermines. The view stretches for a good 40 miles (64 km).

Below: The history of Waterford crystal dates back to 1783 when George and William Penrose founded their crystal manufacturing business in Waterford town. Their aim was to produce 'plain and cut flint glass, useful and ornamental' at their site on Anne Street in the heart of Waterford city – a development which cost £10,000, a staggering figure for the day. Their investment paid off when before long they became Waterford's principal exporters.

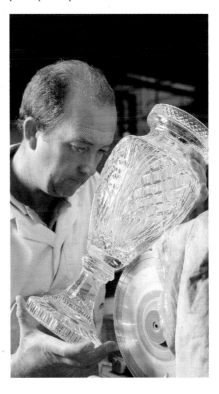

THE PROVINCE OF
ULSTER

A SCATTERED NECKLACE OF thousands of drumlins – small hills of boulder clay, dumped as the last great ice age melted 13,000 years ago – separate the nine counties of the old province of Ulster – Armagh, Antrim, Cavan, Derry, Donegal, Down, Fermanagh, Monaghan and Tyrone – from the rest of the island of Ireland. A natural barrier, it runs in a swathe some 30 miles (48 km) wide from the placid Irish Sea in the east to the Atlantic rollers of the west. Great man-made earthworks, thrown up in the 1st century BC, span the gaps between drumlins. A third barrier, an international border, splits off six of the counties to make Northern Ireland which comprises one sixth of the island and is home to 1.5 million people.

There have been people in Ulster since the Middle Stone Age, over 8000 years ago. They speared salmon, trapped boar and made camp in Ireland's first recorded human settlement – a collection of round huts of woven sapling and deer hide – at Mount Sandel on the banks of the River Bann in County Antrim. The history of this culture, gathered together as the *Ulster Cycle* – the oldest vernacular epic in western European literature – is a heady mix of men, women and gods; battles and lusts; spells and sorrows. It is a history open to interpretation.

The land bridge which once joined Ireland to Britain disappeared around 6000 BC, and it was not until the 4th millennium BC that the next wave of settlers came in the form of Neolithic, New Stone Age farmers who risked the Irish Sea in frail boats of lathe and hide, packed with pigs, cows and sheep, and made landfall among stands of elm – always a sign of good soil – in Strangford Lough.

These new immigrants felled the forests, grew cereals, fired pots, built a distinctively northern style of stone cairn to their gods and buried their dead under the dolmens which stand eternal in many an Ulster field.

Left: The Giant's Causeway, County Antrim. This strange basalt structure was formed by the cooling of molten lava approximately 60 million years ago.

By 2000 BC, in the Bronze Age, contemporary with the pyramids of Egypt's Middle Kingdom and the great Minoan palaces at Knossos on Crete, Ulster's tribes toiled to create the great stone circles of Down and Tyrone, while merchant adventurers taught them to make bronze axe-heads and golden ornaments.

By the coming of the Iron Age, the first Celts had arrived, conquering say some, assimilating say others, those more ancient peoples, the dark-skinned *Fir Bolg*, the red-haired *Tuatha de Dannan*, and the *Cruithin* of Ulster with their warrior-clan structure and their Red Branch Knights. These Gaels welcomed Patrick's Christian mission in the 5th century AD and resisted the subsequent Viking raids on their monasteries in the 8th century. However, in the 12th century the Anglo-Normans took much of Ulster for the English Crown, acting at the behest of Pope Adrian IV.

The Reformation, and Henry VIII's and Elizabeth I's espousal of the Protestant cause, added another dimension. The new colonists were Protestants; the colonized remained Catholic. Eventually England's savage campaigns of attrition paid off and Ulster's Gaelic leaders were exiled to continental Europe, sailing from Donegal in 1607.

England's promotion of the Plantation of Ulster in the 17th century further marginalized the Catholic population by settling the best lands with Protestant Lowland Scots. Begun under James I and VI in 1609, the Plantation suffered severe set-backs in the rebellion of 1641 when many Protestants were massacred; massacres for which the Lord Protector, Oliver Cromwell, took sour revenge in 1649.

In 1690 William of Orange, having accepted the British Crown and representing the forces of Protestantism, defeated James II, a Catholic, at the Battle of the Boyne. This battle and its date are indelibly burned into Ulster's divided psyche, and such complexities as the mid-18th century wave of Presbyterian republican emigration to America and the United Irishmen's Rebellion of 1798, which too had their origins among the north's Protestant non-conformist republicans, are not often weighed in this history's balance in an even-handed manner.

The year of 1916 brought the Easter Rising and 1919 the Declaration of Independence in Dublin and the Irish Republican Army's (IRA) war

Below: William III, King of England, formerly Prince William of Orange, landed at Carrickfergus in County Antrim on 14th June 1690 with a Protestant army to confront the forces of his rival, the ousted King James II who had successfully rallied assistance from his Catholic supporters in Ireland. The first major battle in this power struggle took place at the River Boyne on 1st July (11th July by today's calendar) 1690 and culminated in the first of a series of defeats for the Jacobite forces which would eventually prove fatal for the Catholic cause.

A Prospect of CARRECK-FERGUS.
Being the Place where King William landed in Ireland.

A. The King in the Mary Yacht Capt Collins
B. Prince George in the Henrietta Yacht Capt Sanderson
C. The King goeing a Shoare in Sr Clo: Chouells Barg
D. Sr C Shovell Rear Admll of the Blew in the Monk with his Squadron
Bonfiers on the Shoare.

THE PROVINCE OF ULSTER

against British rule. These were violent times perpetrated by men who had come home from the grim battlefields of the 'Great War' (the First World War, 1914–18) and were accustomed to slaughter. The ranks of the IRA, and of the opposing Ulster Volunteer Force, swelled.

As fears of a civil war in Ulster grew, the British Cabinet devised the 1920 Government of Ireland Act which aimed at imposing a solution without ignoring the demographics of the situation. In 1922 dominion status under the title of Irish Free State (later called Eire) was eventually offered to 26 southern counties. The six northeastern counties of Ulster (those reckoned to have Protestant majorities, whose political allegiance was therefore to a British rather than an Irish state) were retained inside the United Kingdom in an entity thenceforth called Northern Ireland.

In this poem Seamus Heaney describes the uneasy Anglo-Irish relationship in terms of a husband's feelings for his pregnant wife.

> *Your back is a firm line of eastern coast*
> *And arms and legs are thrown*
> *Beyond your gradual hills. I caress*
> *The heaving province where our past has grown.*
> *I am the tall kingdom over your shoulder*
> *That you would neither cajole nor ignore.*
> *Conquest is a lie. I grow older*
> *Conceding your half-independent shore*
> *Within whose borders now my legacy*
> *Culminates inexorably.*

FROM: 'ACT OF UNION' BY SEAMUS HEANEY

Above: Born in Derry in 1939, Seamus Heaney is one of Ireland's leading contemporary poets. While his early work focused mainly on the sectarian atmosphere of rural Derry, his later poems explored the parallels between the violence being perpetrated in Northern Ireland and the ancient sacrificial rites of Jutland, whose victims' bodies were found, perfectly preserved, in Danish bog. In 1995 he won the Nobel Prize for Literature, the fourth Irish writer to do so.

Like many constitutional solutions devised as empires shrink, the 1922 Act was far from perfect. There was one house of representatives in Dublin, and another in Belfast. The great majority of Protestants in Northern Ireland saw their allegiance as being to the British Crown and the government in Westminster; the great majority of Catholics were nationalists with their allegiances in Dublin to a government which would later claim the whole of Ireland as 'the national territory'. Elections to Stormont became a sectarian head count.

Without its 'Troubles' Northern Ireland might well be seen as embodying the essence of a rural neatness the size of Connecticut. Trim hedges and wan limestone walls border its small-holdings. White sheep and dun cows graze the green fields and sturdy farmhouses nestle in clumps of sycamore. Tidy towns are linked by well-metalled roads, their grass verges clipped in orderly precision. Signs point up each historic mound of ancient stone.

In contrast, the roads of Cavan, Monaghan and Donegal wander and camber among the hills. However, while Stormont's Protestant Unionist government undoubtedly built better roads than those in Eire, it saw little wrong in its discriminatory attitude to Catholics. But, the times they were a-changing. In 1968 students protested, not only on the streets of Washington and Paris, but also on those of Belfast and Derry. By 1969 Civil Rights marches were prevalent in the 'six counties'. That year also brought their suppression. The 'Troubles' had begun.

Today, as Ulster's tragic melodrama continues to unfold, the great majority of the population – though still segregated by the sour dance of religion and history – looks on aghast from opposing wings, wishing that peace could bring down the curtain, permanently, on a show which has long outrun any purpose it once had.

ANTRIM

Antrim's Spanish gold

THERE WAS A TIME, in the late 16th century, when there were upwards of 3000 Spaniards in the old province of Ulster, the majority of them making for the castle of Dunluce on Antrim's north coast. They were the survivors of many thousands more shipwrecked when the pride of the invincible Armada of Philip II of Spain foundered off Ireland's western shores.

Philip, married to Mary Tudor and having endured enough harrying from the ships of Mary's half-sister Elizabeth I of England, made it his mission to destroy England's fleet once and for all, thus bringing victory to the cause of Catholic Counter-Reformation. So, on 30th May 1588, his fleet of 141 ships weighed anchor off the port of Lisbon and turned north into the Atlantic.

The English will tell you that it was the commando tactics of the English privateers, operating at long range among and behind the enemy lines under the daring command of naval captains like Francis Drake, which defeated the Armada, while the Spanish maintain that it was the unusually strong equinoxal gales off the Shetland Isles, north of Scotland, which brought the Armada to its sea-sodden knees.

In truth it was a combination of the two. By the time the great ships took shelter off Ireland's windswept western shores they were under-supplied and overloaded – crammed with the soldiery from other ships already sunk.

One of the last ships to go down was the three-masted galleon, *Girona*, which struck a reef off Lacada Point east of Dunluce Castle, near to midnight in late October 1588. She was carrying a complement of 1300 men, just nine of whom survived. It is said that in the darkness their panic-stricken captain mistook the Chimneys in the Giant's Causeway for the real chimneys of Dunluce, whose ruthless commander, Sorley Boye

Left: Dunluce Castle, romantic and exposed, perches on the cliff edge near Port na Spannaigh *near where the Spanish galleon, the* Girona, *sank in 1588.*

Right: In May 1588, the Spanish Armada set sail out of Lisbon under the command of the Duke of Medina Sidonia. It was a substantial force comprising 141 vessels, totalling 62,278 tons with 7666 seamen and 18,529 soldiers.

Below: A gold salamander, encrusted with rubies, which was one of the artefacts salvaged from the Girona *by a team of marine archaeologists 400 years after the ill-fated Spanish galleon sank off the coast of Antrim. This salvage operation was also responsible for one of the most poignant of all recoveries from Spanish wrecks, a slim gold ring depicting a hand holding a heart and inscribed with the immortal words: 'No tengo más que darte' (I have nothing more to give you).*

MacDonnell, was known to be fiercely anti-English.

The wreck left a trail of stone arquebus balls across the ocean floor as well as chestfuls of golden trinkets, much of which MacDonnell would later use to finance the repair of his favoured stronghold.

Other Spanish galleons foundered off the west coast, and many thousands – including the flower of Spain's richest families – perished, broken-limbed on golden beaches. Others fell to the sword, pikes and gallows of the Irish, greedy for plunder. Hundreds, naked, starving, fevered and sick from a diet of wet biscuit and putrified meat, were ridden down by English cavalry.

MacDonnell took his forenames, Sorley Boye, from the Gaelic *Somhaile Buidhe*, the 'summer-soldier, yellow-haired' for the Viking who traditionally raided from the north each summer. He had both Viking and Scots blood in his veins, was Lord of the Western Isles and was among the most astute of the Celtic politicians opposed to Elizabeth I's territorial claims. His family having been driven out of Scotland by the Campbells, Sorley Boye established power in Antrim and made treaties with the O'Neills, the then kings of 'the Great Irishry', so called by the English more out of fear than respect.

In July 1575, Sorley Boye had watched helpless from the mainland as the English put 500 of his clanswomen and their children to the sword on Rathlin Island off the coast of Antrim. Maddened with sorrow, he took his revenge ten years later on New Year's Day 1583, at Bonamargy east of Ballycastle, by burning the Abbey at night and slaughtering until the grass ran red with blood.

The English offered parley, but Sorley Boye and his Redshanks – named thus after their custom of fighting bare-legged even in the winter's frosts – then set out to snatch Dunluce, craftily and bloodily from the English hands. The castle's weakness lay in its constable's taste for his young Scots mistress who was in fact playing Mata Hari for Sorley Boye. On the night of All Hallows she let down a rope and man-sized basket to enable the waiting Redshanks to scale the cliffs and hang the constable from the walls in the basket's place. So Sorley had the castle, but the English had his son's head. They had found him hiding in a freshly dug grave and cut his throat. At the subsequent peace and conciliation talks he was shown his son's head on a pike. 'My son,' he observed chillingly, 'hath many heads.' Not surprisingly, for a man who understood the heart of darkness in other men's souls, he and his descendants, in the end, owned most of the county of Antrim.

Off the coast, west in the setting sun, lies the Donegal peninsula of Inishowen and Ireland's most northerly point, the island of Inishtrahull. East is Rathlin Island which has as yet escaped the manicured tyranny of the golf course. Instead it is rich in the spring and summer with the scent of wild flowers, its lakes speckled with the rings made by tiny brown trout, its blustery shores filled with the cries of the thousands of cliff-breeding sea-birds. However, when the clouds darken the sky, it is too easy to imagine Sorley Boye's anguish as he stood on the mainland, watching his people slaughtered at the place they now call *Crook Ascreidlin*, 'the hill of the screaming'.

South of Ballycastle, one road runs south over the moors, where the buzzards wheel searching for red Irish grouse, and through the market towns of Ballymoney, Ballymena and Antrim, their citizens resigned to being the butt of many jokes concerning their Scots heritage and accent and, allegedly, taut purse strings.

Glenaan, 'the glen of the rushes', ends in Cushendall where Layde Old Church graveyard is calcium-rich with the bones of MacDonnells. Sorley himself is locked, inviolate, as he requested, in a tomb at Bonamargy. At last, had he known the Spanish, he could have said to his people: *No tengo más que darte.*

Below: Glenballyeamon, 'Eamon's glen', one of the nine glens of Antrim, that also include: Glencorp which translates as 'glen of the slaughter'; Glenarm, 'the glen of the army'; Glencloy, 'the glen of the hedges'; Glencriff, 'the glen of the laborer'; Glenaan, 'the glen of the rushes'; Glenshesk, 'the glen of the sedges'; Glentaisie, 'Taisie's glen'; and Glendun, 'the brown glen', where at Castle Carra, Sorley Boye invited his fiercest enemy, Shane 'The Proud' O'Neill, to dinner, slit his throat and then presented his head on a pike to Elizabeth I.

ARMAGH

Ulster's flowery vale

Hɪsᴛᴏʀʏ, ʟᴇɢᴇɴᴅ ᴀɴᴅ ᴍʏᴛʜ combine to provide the epic of the golden-haired princess Macha, who dominated the times in which she lived, becoming, for the Celts, their goddess of lusts and wars for 1000 years from 700 ʙᴄ onwards. In one of her many guises she married Nemhedh, a darkly handsome mercenary come lately from Scythia, northeast of the Black Sea, and later died at the top of the forest hill he cleared for her giving the hill its name: *Ard Macha*, 'Macha's Height', Armagh.

To the west, Navan Fort is all that remains of the ancient capital of Ulster where, at *An Eamain* or 'Macha's twins', in another guise, another of Macha's husbands, Cruinnuig, forced his wife – who could allegedly run like the wind – to race against the horse of Connor, King of Ulster. Pregnant, Macha begged him to postpone the race, but he refused at the cost of her life. Having won, Macha died giving birth to twins, cursing as she did so the men of Ulster to suffer the pains of childbirth.

Macha's city, Armagh itself, sits on two hills, with the Catholic and Protestant cathedrals facing each other across a valley. Protestant St Patrick's stands where the pragmatic saint, conscious of the area's political and religious significance, built his second church in 444 ᴀᴅ. It must have looked its best at the end of the 18th century when it was restored by Armagh's own Francis Johnston, the man who gave the city, and so much of Dublin, its Georgian charms. Now, Johnston's delicate touches stand defaced by lesser talents, its orangey sandstone exterior forbidding, the carved heads grim in their frieze.

The cathedral tower affords a fine perspective over the medieval town, with its narrow streets coiling up the cathedral hill. Across the valley the 39-peal carillon and the exuberant Byzantine interior of twin-spired St Patrick's Catholic Church attest to the success of the 19th century primate cardinals in charge of the original financing. In the wave of

Left: Where Navan Fort stood in 700 ʙᴄ, at the centre of the old capital of Ulster, there is now a moody, cloud-shadowed, hill-top enclosure.

Above: Once a racecourse, Armagh city's Georgian Mall is shaped like a cricket bat, a fitting design for a place where the thunder of horses hooves has long since been replaced by the echo of leather on willow.

compassion which swept Europe in the wake of Ireland's Great Famine even the emperors of France and Austria found it in their hearts to support the cathedral's fund-raising bazaar in 1865 – from which a long-case clock still awaits collection by its purchaser. The red hats of all its cardinals hang, with some pomp, inside.

For an understanding of the key role that the Church has played in Armagh's history, you only have to walk through the wonderful, tree-lined, Georgian Mall. Many of its encompassing limestone buildings are a testament to the architect, Johnston, and his sponsor Archbishop Robinson, harking back to a time when clerics were rich and sure patrons of the arts. There were few advisory committees then; few bureaucrats; few rapacious consultants.

At the south end of the Mall stands the old gaol, now minus gallows; at the north end Johnston's 1809 Court House. On the east stands the one-time schoolhouse, which is now the delightfully arcane Armagh County Museum. How improving it must have been for the school's pupils to be pulled by the ears and lined up in ranks to watch malfeasants, hobbling in irons from north to south to be held for deportation or worse. How reassuring for townhouse residents looking down from their elegant balconies.

The acerbic Jonathan Swift, who seems to have enjoyed escaping his duties as a Dublin dean, often came north, staying on occasion with the Achesons at their manor house in south Armagh – 'bandit country' to the English tabloids during the 'Troubles'. While old Sir Archibald Acheson, the county sheriff, was a dull stick, strong on public colonial virtues, his young wife, Anne, it seems, was quite the reverse. To his satisfaction, prosperous obscurity was how the sheriff deemed his own life, mindless it seems of the poor, starving on the village edge. It was a situation meat for Swift's satirical pen, and indeed he chased off a dozen or so poems mostly mocking M'Lady's concerns for her ageing coquettish house guest, who dallied with her over cards into the small hours, and made so free with her house and garden, if not, as far as is discreetly recorded, her physical affections.

Further verses for Lady Anne were quite scatological in the details of the functioning of the outdoor privies Swift ordered built for her comfort. However, Swift's concerns stretched well beyond the confines of Lady Anne's hospitality. He criticized the emigration to America forced upon so many of his Ulster Scots Presbyterian neighbours. Not that he tolerated their religion, but more he recognized the contribution to the relative stability of the early 18th century Ulster economy made by their Calvinist work ethic. He contrasted the relative wealth of the north with the appalling poverty in southern counties, though he wrote of himself 'as a stranger in a strange land', and he spoke of 'three terrible years dearth of corn, and every place strowed with beggars'. For even in prosperous Armagh, the poor were always with him.

By all accounts he was happy in Armagh, that is until Sir Archibald finally woke up to his 'frolick' with Lady Anne. It was in the wake of this scandal, rebuffed by society and exasperated by what he perceived as the government's economic follies, that Swift wrote *A Modest Proposal*, his most famous and savage of satires, in which he recommends the eating of Ireland's starving children, thus turning them into an economic asset. Soon after Swift's final visit to Markethill, Lady Anne left her husband for ever, and went to live with her mother.

County Armagh was also the birthplace of the Protestant Orange Order which was founded in 1795. Today, members of the Order,

Below: This limestone doorway in the city of Armagh exemplifies the uniquely satisfying traditions of Irish Georgian architecture of which elegance, simplicity and style are the key features.

Above: A veteran takes part in contemporary Orange Day celebrations.

Left : The Twelfth of July in Portadown *(painting by Sir John Lavery).*
Orangemen's Day celebrates William of Orange's victorious Irish campaign.

wearing their distinctive orange sashes, march across Northern Ireland on 12th July each year, and often, in contentious rehearsal, several weekends beforehand. 'Flashpoint Feared' run the anticipatory headlines. Many republican Catholics see such marches as provocatively supremacist, and while some marchers delight in this shrewd observance, others would prefer that these parades be regarded simply as colourful celebrations of folk history, as unthreatening as New Orleans' *Mardi Gras*, and surely to be welcomed in a province not given much to dancing in the streets.

In mid-August, in rituals not dissimilar – banners billowing in the Armagh breezes – the members of the Catholic Nationalist Ancient Order of Hibernians also march to the accordion, fife and drum. In truth, only the slogans and narrative paintings on the huge banners and the icons on the green, rather than orange, sashes distinguish matters for a stranger.

Away from politics, Armagh is best savoured listening to the music in its *uillean* pipers' clubs; following its road-bowls champions along high-hedged lanes; walking through its Bramley apple orchards in May; or by just sitting on a wall in Armagh's Mall, gentle evening breeze tugging at the chestnut blossom, while white flannelled sportsmen, out there between the ranks of historic cannon, play leisurely cricket on its green, green grass.

BELFAST

City of pubs and churches

BELFAST NOW, sitting in a saucer of green hills astride the currently-being-gentrified River Lagan, is a medium-sized, post-industrial, Victorian city with a surfeit of engaging pubs, architecturally extravagant churches, and an improbable number of street-level car parks.

Making the world's headlines with harrowing regularity, Belfast is remarkable and compelling principally because it is the war zone for a few hundred violent activists from two opposing religions, from a fistful of blue collar enclaves, who for the last 25-plus years have resolutely defied the massed powers of the British Crown. Since 1968 more than 3000 people have died: shot; blown to bloody fragments; garrotted; bludgeoned; burned; and countless more exhausted by grief. Since then electronic images of their deaths have spun outwards, endlessly, into the expanding universe.

During the badland times of the early 1970s the few strangers here were journalists and soldiers. Good citizens rushed home from work, if they had any, and the only people on the night-time streets were the police, the hacks, the army and the revolutionaries and counter-revolutionaries. The place had a bizarre romance. Bars closed soon after dark, disgorging television crews, assassins, racketeers, touts, informers and spies from a dozen nations back onto the cracked and drizzled pavements. Barristers and solicitors, who were then the new rich, dined well in a shifting geography of small and sometimes eccentric restaurants.

Over the years, a certain number, bombed or burned out from their ghettos, or in general fear of such assaults, moved as refugees to quiet country towns. However, since the first days of the brokered peace in the summer of 1994, the mood has been cautiously robust. The city, where the streetwise greeting has always been ''bout ye?', an abbreviation of 'How's about you?', has never lost its ironic confrontational sense of

Left: Built in response to Queen Victoria's charter of 1888 which gave Belfast its city status, the magnificent City Hall dominates the heart of the city.

humour, nor its mendicant economy so heavily dependent on American, British and EU subsidy. It burgeons with cafés, theme pubs, ethnic eateries and the cool fashionable restaurants of media-chefs, all packed with visiting social anthropologists, incognito Hollywood stars researching superficial scripts and the even newer rich, the cohorts of the new local industries of peace and reconciliation.

Post-stress monitoring, conflict consultancy, social engineering, and empowerment of the socially disenfranchised are among the specialities. These optimistic agencies are staffed in the main by the well-funded, the self-promoting, and the often self-appointed, taking their cheques from the United States of America and the EU, from Canada, the perpetually concerned Scandinavians and from Britain itself. Their members have lives more fulfilling than those whom they would comfort.

Unemployment, outside these new and fashionable conceits is still unacceptably high. The much lauded and welcomed visits of presidents and rock stars bring the city's citizens the well-deserved glow of media attention, but whether these public delights create long-term benefit is still to be assessed and segregation by religion in voting-ward and in education persists.

The politics of peace aside, for the enquiring visitor there isn't an engaging taxi driver in the city who hasn't an explanation for each withering kerbside wreath; each gable-end political mural with its Balaclavaed heroes, dove of peace in one hand and Kalashnikov in the other; each bombed out gap in a street's architecture.

Right: A mural in Belfast proclaims the benefits of peace. However, despite the thousands of hours of high-profile discussions, Catholics and Protestants still attend different schools and live in separate ghettos, whether in redbrick, serried rows on housing estates or in the leafy suburbs of south Belfast. At the time of writing, the Shankill voting ward, an enclave in nationalist West Belfast has 3856 Protestants and 39 Catholics while adjoining Ardoyne has 5686 Catholics and 31 Protestants.

The city's affluent middle-classes, and its not-so-affluent youth, seek their urban pleasures in a narrow southern-facing triangle of streets – styled over-optimistically as The Golden Mile – taking as its base a line from the solid Victorian confidence of the City Hall to the foxed charm of the Old Museum Arts Centre. The triangle's apex is located just past the curvilinear delights of the Botanic Gardens' Palm House in the prosperous University suburbs.

Within these confines are found the art galleries, arts festivals, bars, bistros, cafés, charity shops, launderettes, museums, opera houses, pizza parlours, restaurants, sandwich bars and theatres thought necessary for middle class life.

But curiously, for a city with such a confrontational sense of its own presence, the people of Belfast have no generic title, as have Bostonians, Dubliners, Glaswegians, Londoners and Parisians. Belfastonians? Belfasters? Belfastians? None have the confident ring of acceptance. However, the citizens do have numerous rituals. For instance, they will show every one of their visitors the tiles and stained glass of the Victorian Crown Liquor Saloon, an interior which has made it, in effect, a national monument. If that is too crowded they will lead the way to nearby Robinson's, Morrison's, The Spinner's and Dempsey's, all pubs which attempt – with varying degrees of success – to recreate the Irish rural past of village spirit grocers and small-town gentleman's book-lined clubs.

Graduate migrants, who left years ago because of the 'Troubles' return to Lavery's Gin Palace comforted to find its customers caught in the same 1960s time warp. The more emboldened may find themselves in the Empire, a deconsecrated church, where 'in your face' stand-up comedy offers a rare insight into the city's mood. For it is a truism that adversity and fear produce the best jokes.

Reading the city's current frame of mind from its media is a harder job. During the bad times, journalists and management on the three daily newspapers, one overtly nationalist, one primarily unionist, one trying to be somewhere in between, covered the complexities of the stubborn brutalities and conspiracies with admirable impartiality.

But just as the new peace, when it came, caught the traffic planners severely off guard (they had not had to worry about traffic jams for a quarter of a century), it also placed new burdens on the media.

When news was brought to the journalists' keyboards by the very

Above: Children play in the Catholic enclave of Ardoyne in North Belfast. Both here and in the Protestant enclave of Shankill, strangers are welcome enough, though the question as to what specifically a quarter of a century of bomb, bullet and mayhem has achieved should be put with some circumspection.

Below: George Augustus Chichester, the 2nd Marquis of Donegall (1769–1844), Belfast's wildly improvident landlord whose extravagant debts forced him to alienate his lands by means of perpetual leases from the 1820s.

sound of the bomb itself, by the flame lighting up the nightscape outside the newsroom, by the bombers' coded telephone call, by a paramilitary group's faxed claim and politician's faxed counter-claim, peace can leave holes in the news menu.

Some lacunae have been filled by new terrors. Female and male rape; drug-associated killings; attacks on the elderly; ex-terrorist guns for hire; punishment maimings, and, newly revealed after having been bravely and doggedly researched, the appalling history of child sexual abuse inside the Catholic church.

With regard to 'good news' the feeling prevails that it is churlish – for the moment anyway – to question anything which might herald peace and prosperity. So while the arrival of a massive chainstore creates 300 jobs and is hailed as a sign of acceptance into the canon of western affluence, little thought is given to the family-owned stores which will fold in consequence.

The real city begins just north of The Golden Mile. Here, where the feel-good factor reigns supreme, customers sipping pints in the Kitchen Bar, Bittle's Bar, The Morning Star and White's Tavern, will speak with the voice of an older Belfast. The same voice would be heard, too, in the city-village suburbs where hairdressers' establishments don't yet have weakly punning names, and spades and garden forks are still stacked on the pavement each morning outside family-owned general stores, whose stock-in-trade still speaks of rural–urban links, not yet broken, of small gardens, of allotments, and of summer barbecues.

Among the middle classes, many of whom have seen bombs only through the filter of television, the new mood is confident. The new and circular Waterfront Hall speaks for restored civic pride. Plans for riparian stadia, science parks, a national gallery, pile up in planners' offices.

Service industries prosper. Pavements are refurbished, the street furniture is new and international, the trading names in the shopping malls of Donegal Place and Royal Avenue, the city's major commercial boulevards, are those of any British high street.

A few hundred years ago there was little here except a rough castle by an estuary sandbank. Choir boys fished for salmon in the Lagan,

apprentices complained of too many oysters in their diet. In time the linen and shipbuilding trades would make the city rich and polluted, supplying its merchants with the money to create its solid but decorative Victorian architecture for their businesses, the cramped rows of redbrick houses and mean streets for their workers, and the city parks for the orderly and educational enjoyment of their tradespeople.

Since those industries atrophied, this city, like many others in this European archipelago, has had to struggle for its new wealth. Further back in history its aetiology can be read in the legacies of two men, one an hereditary toff, the other an architect, opportunist and politican. One sold Belfast, the other built it. Such were the financial irresponsibilities of the 2nd Marquis of Donegall that he had seen the inside of a debtor's prison before he inherited the whole city in 1799. Thereafter, so profligate was his lifestyle that, after his death in 1844, his son's advisors had to sell what was left of his inheritance to pay off the family's debts, thus opening up Lagan's banks to bankers and industrialists.

Stability was assured by Charles Lanyon, the most prosperous industrialist of them all who among other things gave the city an architectural language that all of its citizens could understand. His banks borrowed their vernacular from the houses of the medieval merchant princes of Italy. His church spires soared towards God. His prison's bulk put fear into so many hearts, his towering Courts of Justice intimidated the miscreant, his viaducts carried the railways, his tree plantations made solid the shifting bogland.

By his Queen's Bridge, named for Queen Victoria, he gave the city the Custom House and what is now the First Trust Bank, plus the Northern Bank in Waring Street nearby. Meanwhile, the New House of Correction (now Crumlin Road Prison) and the equally imposing Court House provided intimidating symbols of law and order.

So the student newly arrived in Belfast would do well to take a walk on this unofficial 'Lanyon Trail', before sitting down among the bookcased and leathered delights of the Linenhall Library to begin, yet another, doctorate on yet one more aspect of the heritage of the 'Troubles'.

Above top: Queen's University, built by Lanyon in 1849, is a redbrick replica of Magdalen College, Oxford.

Above: Sir Charles Lanyon (1813–89), was Belfast's most important architect during the 19th century. He was also a ruthless property speculator, an engineer, a Conservative politician and a 'ladies' man' who married the boss's daughter and became mayor of Belfast.

CAVAN

County of lakes and waterways

JUST AS THE OLD MEN, pipe smoking dark tobacco in public houses in County Down, oblige with the fiction that there is one island in Strangford Lough for every day of the year, those in County Cavan will proffer you the obverse. Cavan, a lakeland labyrinth, has, they boast, a lake in the county for each and every day of the 365. A 'disappearing' one, over a limestone sump, takes its curtain call each leap year.

Fanciful or not, it is a description which will suffice for the county's fortunes, precarious enough at times, and its principal legends have water at their fount. At its centre is a scatter of lakes linked by waterways natural and unnatural.

The 250 mile-long (402 km) Shannon, Ireland's greatest river, and major provider both of the country's indigenous hydro-electric power, and its water-based tourism, has its source in the moistness of the western slopes of Cuilcagh Mountain. Here, water sparkles down in the deep pool under the lichen-covered trees and the river, which takes its name from *Sionna*, grand-daughter of *Lir*, the god of the seas, begins its journey to the Atlantic. Meanwhile it neighbour, the River Erne, rises near Crosskeys and flows first south, then, in Lough Gowna, turns north towards Fermanagh's two broad lakes, Upper and Lower Lough Erne.

In the mid-19th century the proximity of these two rivers, the Shannon and the Erne, inspired the construction of the ill-planned Ballinamore–Ballyconnell Canal which it was hoped would complete the circuit of commercial canals that was to link Dublin to Belfast. However, this was never to be. As the budget overran, as canal budgets always seemed to, several economies of scale were made: depth was reduced to just over 3 feet (1 m), while canal towpaths, which were expensive to construct, were maintained despite the patent impossibility of operating a horse-tow across the wider lakes. By the time the canal was completed

Left: As a result of pesticides and other modern farming methods the 'crek-crek' call of the male corncrake, once common, is no longer heard in Cavan.

63

Right: 'Mermen discovered in Lough Oughter in County Cavan by the Belfast Naturalist Field Club.'
This 'joke photograph', so captioned, was taken around the turn of the century by the Belfast photographer, R.J. Welch.

in 1860, having taken 14 years to build, a sad catalogue of penny-pinching, mismanagement and general ineptitude had rendered it virtually unusable and certainly no match for the increasingly commercial railway companies.

From the minute it was officially opened, water leaked from locks, banks caved and when what would be the last boat to do so passed through its locks in 1936, it took three weeks. Official records show that only eight boats had paid tolls on the 36 mile (58 km) journey, in either direction, in the 76 years since construction had been completed.

Today, in a period of post-industrial nostalgia and increasing leisure time, there is a burgeoning desire to observe – gin and tonic in hand – the manicured outdoors and the remnants of that once labour-intensive environment. The European Commission has funded much of the re-opening of the Ballinamore–Ballyconnell Canal, now promoted – logically, but with little eye for the nuances of nostalgia with which its attractions are imbued – as the Shannon–Erne Waterway.

The massive, hand-chiselled locks tower over the boats as always, but a credit card-like device allows captains-for-the-week, piloting their shallow, plastic-skinned hire-cruisers, to operate the huge wooden lock gates by sweatless and silent electric power. Bankside alder, willow, hazel, flag iris, watchful heron and dipping grebe accustom themselves to the habits of these new invaders of their once-silent water world.

If Cavan had a county song, there would be none better than 'An Bonnán Buí', 'The Song of the Yellow Bittern', written by the 18th-century poet Cathal Mac Giolla Ghunna and remembered in stone in Blacklion. Now bittern, cuckoo and corncrake are gone, driven out by pesticides, soil enrichment, the draining of callows and watermeadows and the early cutting of grass for silage. On both sides of the border, bird protection agencies offer – to little avail – subsidies to farmers who will cut hay late to enable the secretive corncrake to rear its young in peace.

Below: The disappearance of the corncrake – once a frequent winter visitor – from many parts of Ireland has evoked an impassioned campaign by bird conservation groups to try and encourage farmers to engage in 'corncrake-friendly farming'.

Now every lakeshore is dotted with the discreet green of the umbrellas of Dutch, English, French and German fishermen, and farm houses, turned 'Bed and Breakfast' (B&B), install 'picture windows', crazy-paved patios and barbecue pits and scatter their beds with duvets.

The multitudes of tiny pubs are still held in family names, the shop fronts are mostly still clear of the 1970s garishness so beloved of men of small commerce in most other Irish counties. On garage forecourts and on the factory floor premises of the local light industries, 'Country and

Irish' – a more lachrymose version of Country and Western – music, echoes tinnily across the wavelengths.

On the wooden pub counter, the local paper offers pictures of weddings and priests; of roughly-suited, factory-sponsored brass bands in the local festival and of shop re-fittings. There are court reports to pore over: of farmers caught without road tax; of the results of planning appeals. Old men speak slowly, courteous enough but secretive; the younger debase their badinage with an excess of expletives. Everybody smokes and on the bumpy bog roads between the towns, turf smoke filters into everyone's cars.

Turn on the car radio and there is a dedication from nearby Ballyjamesduff.

> Oh, the grass it is green around Ballyjamesduff,
> And the blue sky is over it all;
> And tones that are tender, and tones that are gruff,
> Are whispering over the sea.
> 'Come back, Paddy Reilly, to Ballyjamesduff,
> Come home, Paddy Reilly, to me.'

FROM: 'COME BACK PADDY REILLY' BY PERCY FRENCH (1854–1920)

I'm not sure the fastidious Percy would have liked it sung Country and Western style.

Above: Increasingly popular with holiday-makers, the Shannon–Erne Waterway fairly groans with barges and 'pleasure cruisers' during the summer months.

DERRY

History's fulcrum

ERRY, THE MOST COMPLETE of Ireland's walled cities, and the administrative and emotional heartland of the county of Derry, has more than once played a pivotal role in European history. While the city's strategic position on a hill overlooking one of Ireland's largest rivers has long made it a sought-after prize for ambitious warriors, prelates, carpetbaggers and politicians, its sobriquet, 'the Maiden City', attests to the three centuries its walls have stood inviolate.

In the early centuries of Christendom, a monastery – with its many trades and centre of administration – was the nearest thing Ulster had to a town. So Columba, also known as Columcille, a prolific founder of monasteries who built his first here in 546 AD, is regarded as Derry's founder. He built high on an island hill just off the left bank of the estuary of the plenteous River Foyle, pragmatically choosing an oak grove for his setting. The grove had previously been a place of pagan worship and the saint's men were canny enough not to chop down too many trees when they built, for oak has always had a particular resonance in Irish mythology.

Doire, pronounced near enough 'Derry', is Irish for 'oak grove ' and the sessile oak, *Quercus petraea*, is one of the great mythical trees of the island, lending to the early Irish runic ogham script its sign for 'D', from *dair* for 'oak'.

Having survived as an important Christian stronghold, Derry featured heavily in Henry II's plan to annex Ireland in the 12th century. He had a powerful ally in the form of Rome which had had enough of the independent Irish church, so, with Pope Adrian IV's approval, Henry himself led an invasion in October 1171. In 1177 he despatched the much-feared Somerset knight, John de Courcy, and a force of Anglo-Normans north to take Ulster, that most recalcitrant of provinces. The

Left: Musicians playing at a music festival in County Derry. Known as fleadhs, *these festivals take place all over Ireland during the summer months.*

Irish proved to be little match for his mailed knights, Flemish crossbowmen, Welsh longbowmen, and de Courcy ringed the coast with stout castles; two are still standing at Dundrum and Carrickfergus. However, in the end the wilds of the county defeated him and so Derry survived as the Irish powerbase and focus of the Columban monasteries.

Over the next few centuries, siege and repulse came and went until 1566 when the English forces at last took the city, installing men and munitions in the ancient Christian temple, *Teampull Mhor*. However, the arsenal exploded the following year and the garrison fled.

In 1613, to stabilize the situation, James I took the advice of Sir Thomas Phillips, a plausible Welsh adventurer with lands at Coleraine, to bring the city and surrounding lands under the control of the livery companies of the City of London. Uneasy though the alliance was – the land was still the domain of resentful Irish chiefs and unruly woodkern – all parties agreed and set up what amounted to a joint stock company, not unlike the one that was currently settling the Virginias.

While it was a decision they lived to regret, thus it was that Derry gained the prefix 'London', a form of address used infrequently now by any but the most ardent loyalist.

Somewhat reluctantly, the livery companies – officially referred to as 'undertakers' – established several settlements: the Roe Valley to the

Below: Londonderri *(etching by or in the style of Romeyn de Hooghe). The siege by James II's forces on the blockaded city of Londonderry did not begin until April 1689, five months after the city gates had been closed. It lasted until 28th July when a Protestant fleet, owing allegiance to William III, finally managed to sail through the artillery fire of the Jacobite forces into the quay just below the city, thus liberating the besieged citizens. after eight long months.*

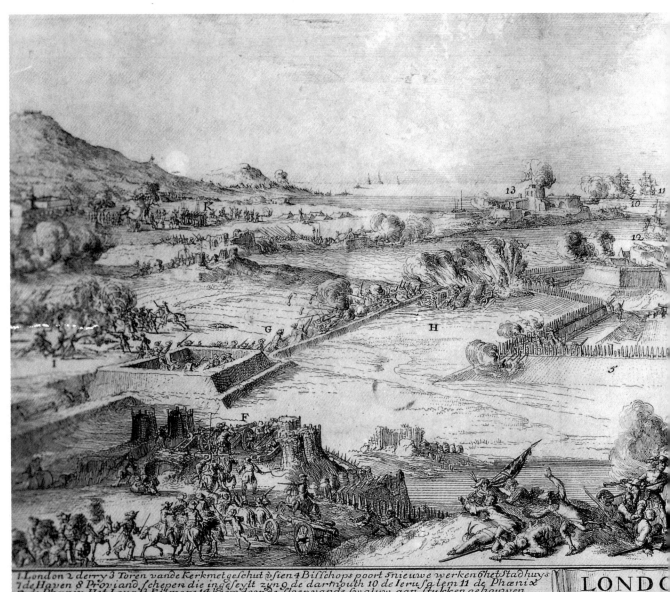

Haberdashers, the Fishmongers and Skinners; the Bann to the Clothmakers, Merchant Tailors, Ironmongers, Mercers, Vintners and Salters; and the Foyle to the Goldsmiths, Cordwainers, Paint-stainers and Armourers as well as the Grocers. Meanwhile, Phillips had Limavady all for himself.

The conditions laid out in the Printed Book of Agreement were tough. However, few shared the king's grand design for an Ireland pacified by investment, viewing it instead as simply another scheme by the Crown to raise their taxes and they made little effort to honour promises to build stone forts, schoolhouses and churches or to deport all Celts of fighting age to Connacht. England, by this time, had been deforested so there was a ready market for barrel staves and ships' timbers. While the colonisers skimped, cutting down the great oaks for profit rather than for building, Irishmen, who should have been deported, were kept as tenants on poor uplands, a cheaper solution than importing settlers from England.

In 1619 the Crown reacted strongly to this defiance, decreeing that unless the 'undertakers' agreed to pay double the taxes their lands would be forfeited. Sullenly they paid. However, in 1635, the new king, Charles I, who shared little of his father's enthusiasm for an Irish colony, summoned the companies, conjoined as the still extant The Honourable The Irish Society, before the Court of Star Chamber and ordered them to

Above: Derry was the last fortified town to be built in Ireland and its city walls, completed in 1618, are some of the best preserved of any in Europe.

RI A *Kirke met de vloot na uch seylende* B *uch* C *yren door die van uch overvallen* D *verse approche* E *Uitval op de yeren en die op geslagen* F *franse begonne werken* G *franse aproches* H *franse werken geruineert* I *franse en yrenhant gemeen* K *vreedheden van K Iacob en d'Avaux tegen de Predicanten* L *franse geslagen*

Above: By Mount Sandel, 8000 year-old seashell middens attest to Ireland's first immigrants.

Right: The Sperrin Mountains are one of Ulster's main sheep farming regions.

give up their lands once and for all. Luckily for the companies, this blatant show of royal autocracy added to the disquiet about royal judgment felt by England's increasingly pro-republican parliamentarians, thus setting the power of two cities, London and Derry, against the Crown and ultimately sparking the English Civil War (1642–49). It would not be the first, nor last, time that Derry would play a key role in European history.

Twice during the 1640s the city walls held out against Irish attacks, and twice the city was held by Protestant parliamentarians against Royalist besiegers. However, the most famous siege of all came almost 40 years later while Catholic James II fought Protestant William III, formerly Prince of Orange, for the British throne.

The citizens of Derry were mainly Scots and English Protestant planters and although William was Dutch, and his army financed mainly by Rome's Pope Innocent XI, the majority of Derry's settlers supported him. On 18th December 1688 a handful of Protestant apprentices, the student class of their day, shut Ferryquay Gate and did not open it until 28th July 1689. Inside the walls, 7000 of the 30,000 townsfolk died from hunger and pestilence. Rats were a shilling a head, but the city's resolve did not falter. Under pressure the defenders hoisted a crimson banner signifying 'No Surrender' which is still the cry of the Protestant Orangemen parading the province every year on 12th July. The siege tied up Jacobite forces, and so helped crown the man who became William III, turning, yet again, the tide of European history.

Today, elegant Georgian doorways decorate the hilly streets; The Honourable The Irish Society is still a major landowner. The elegant spire of Protestant St Columb's Cathedral, built by The Society between 1628 and 1633 in what is known as the 'Planters' Gothic' style, dominates the old city. Outside the walls are the sectarian enclaves: the tiny Protestant Fountain area and sprawling Catholic Bogside, the latter a no-go area for British troops during much of the recent 'Troubles'. On the Bogside's edge, a gable wall reads, 'You are now entering Free Derry'. Of course, this is a sentiment with far reaching implications which would find a large number of opponents both in the city and much further afield. But then Derry must be used to that by now.

DONEGAL

Edge of the known world

O N A GOOD DAY the Donegal air is bright and salty and as fresh as if it had been scrubbed by the very Atlantic. A roar of breakers funnels up the valleys from crescents of untrodden golden sands. A buzzard quarters high in the blue; a dipper darts under the bubbling stream, here, on what was once the edge of the known world. But on a bad day, when winter rain lashes its pot-holed village streets, Donegal sees itself as a lost county, cut off from and ignored by Dublin. When, in 1920, an elaborate constitutional 'solution' to the 'Irish Problem' was enacted by offering dominion status to a 26-county Irish Free State and Home Rule to the six northeastern counties (Antrim, Armagh, Down, Fermanagh, Derry and Tyrone), the three other counties of the old province of Ulster (Cavan, Donegal and Monaghan) were separated off and joined in the new dominion.

The economy they joined was subsequently drained by civil war, and they were the far counties on the new state's periphery. Neutrality during the Second World War, plus high trade tariffs and state censorship, led to economic and social lethargy and further isolation, even after Eire become a Republic in 1948. The whole of the country, and particularly the western counties, remained trapped in some 1930s time warp well into the 1950s, and even today there is a certain amount of catching up still to do.

But many in the Northern Ireland part of Ulster prefer it that way. Belfast's chattering classes scour the lonely valleys and the steep-streeted villages with their tiny ocean harbours, seeking out near derelict cottages to preserve in aspic. Soon turf is once again stacked by the wall, green wellies by the door, Chardonnay in the gas-powered fridge, Irish music among the Mozart CDs. The bungalow rash, scattered high on far hilltops too windy for comfort, their condensation-shrouded picture

Left: A cottage nestles at the base of Muckish Mountain which dominates the northwest of Donegal, appearing from certain aspects like a great ship's prow.

Right: At home in the Blue Stack Mountains in County Donegal, this hill farmer enjoys few of the comforts of 20th century living. He was brought up in these mountains with Irish as his first language and is the only one of his fifteen brothers and sisters still to be living in Donegal, the rest having all long since emigrated.

Above: Soda bread, pronounced 'sohdy' in the vernacular, is a speciality particularly associated with Ireland's northern counties.

Below: An abandoned church in the Poisoned Glen, so called because of a deadly plant that grows there. Of the genus Euphorbia, *this plant has a milky but highly poisonous juice which has rendered the valley water undrinkable. It is said that, as a result, no birds can live there.*

windows leaking blue television-given light, is much deplored.

In a circle of jagged rocks which makes up the tiny bay, the Atlantic boils, rolling white stones as big and as round as cannonballs. A waist-high iron winch, used long ago to haul the lobster boats, rusts amongst the sea-pinks. For the holiday-home hunting family from Northern Ireland, negotiating through the parish priest has secured the agreement of all the descendants – now spread from Boston to Sydney – to sell an abandoned property. A four-wheel drive vehicle stands high over the sheep-cropped grass.

Some – mostly tweed-suited painters and poets – bought cottages decades ago; others might also have established their second home earlier but, over the years of the 'Troubles', there were stories of IRA hardmen in safe havens in Donegal's border villages; of 'northern' registered cars vandalized. Many cut back on their Donegal holidays; others, the more staunchly Unionist, rejected altogether a state they saw as soft on terrorism. But now they are back, crowding the bars with north Down accents; tapping their feet with the fiddlers and playing golf over the sheep-studded links.

The secret of sexing breakfast in Donegal's unsophisticated eating houses – where lunch is dinner, and high tea is the best of the evening meals – is soon revealed: a 'gentleman's' has two eggs, a 'lady's' only one. Outside, the sun sparkles and the heather purples on the valley's slopes. Lamb graze up as far as the screeline; their cutlets, were they on offer, would taste of wild sage and bog mint. The soda and potato breads, if they had not been store-bought, would have been delicious. But, ironically, it is only in the 'big houses', now turned into expensive guesthouses, where the mistress of the house bakes the peasant breads once reserved for servants and stirs the home-made jams fresh from summer hedgerows. Indeed, but for these oases of newly commercialised 'auld dacency', and for a handful of bistros catering – in Derry's Donegal hinterland – for the Maiden City's *nouveau riche*, few restaurants offer the chance to savour the riches of Donegal's coastline: oysters snuggling

in coves, carpets of mussels in inshore beds, crab, crayfish, squat-lobster and shrimp taken in pots whose floats dot the choppy indigo seas. For the majority of diners the choice remains undistinguished – sirloin steak, fried chicken, bland farmed salmon – while in the county's little ports and in the massive overcrowded harbour of Killybegs, where Victorian architecture stands uneasily in the Klondyke atmosphere of a frontier town, thousands of tonnes of fresh brill, dab, haddock, hake, herring, mackerel, monkfish, plaice, ray, scad, skate, sprat, squid, and turbot are landed almost every week.

Yet more is transferred, creaking and rocking, onto 'mother ships' bound for other lands. Over 90 per cent is destined for export: to glisten in boxes in Rungis market in Paris, on the marble slabs of the Maravillas market-house in Madrid, or to be salted, frozen and dried for the canneries of Lagos. Apologists explain the native neglect of fish as a folk memory of the Great Famine, or as a response to the church's insistence on a meatless Friday. For the Church's writ is still large here, and each summer 15,000 barefooted souls spend three days and nights in the 1500 year-old ritual penance of St Patrick's Purgatory on Station Island in Lough Derg, subsisting on a diet of water, black tea and dry bread.

Up the slopes, faint patterns point to transhumance where the sod-roofed 'booleys' stood. Once, many in the county had three homes: a hut by the shore for when diving tern told of inshore herring; a stream-side winter cottage; and a 'booley' used at autumn grazing. Not entirely unlike the county's Northern Ireland visitors: roughing in Donegal at weekends, renting in Mediterranean hills during the summer.

Above: Social anthropologists offer various explanations for the lack of fish in the Donegal diet. Certainly one doesn't have to look that far back in history for a time when fishing gear was roughly made and boats so badly equipped that fishermen drowned all too frequently. Even today, too many boats and their crews are lost off Donegal's shores every year.

DOWN

St Patrick's county

THOUGH THE MAN HIMSELF is all of Ireland's apostle saint, St Patrick's Day is not much celebrated in the northern counties. A few tired bunches of what may be shamrock, normally imported from the Netherlands, are sold over florists' counters. Some take a holiday in solidarity with the Republic's national saint; others stay steadfastly at their desks, shunning such 'Roman' fripperies. Well before the multinational hypermarkets started spreading the word according to Mammon and greedily eroding the concept of the universal holiday, uncertainty about allegiances cast a doubt over the whole proceedings.

Even in Downpatrick, the saint's supposed burial place, his day's commemorations – a motley parade of school bands and 'floats', prominently sponsored by local business men – have neither the penitential nor the colourful vigour which are applied to local saints' days in southern European countries. The parade's defenders will offer up that perennial Irish excuse, 'Sure wouldn't it be grand? If only we had the weather.'

Aside from the rain the suspicion exists in Ireland that St Patrick's Day is really a matter for Americans whose celebrations – beer dyed grass green in South Boston; a bilious river in Chicago; a jolly, if anachronistic, parade in New York – stretch over almost a week. Thus Irish passport holders, north and south of the border, who are affluent enough – or whose employers connive at business meetings located in America in mid-March – fly west on Aer Lingus, celebrating all the way there and back in a sentimental miasma of Irish Americana. Accountants, one presumes, look the other way.

For many it comes as a surprise, perhaps, that our Irish saint was the son of a Roman official, Calpurnius, based in Wales, and that his efforts to proselytize among the then native inhabitants of this island were

Left: Strangford Lough and its 'pladdies' or islands, where Patrick landed in 432 AD, were so named six centuries later by the invading Vikings.

Below: St Patrick (painting by Sir John Lavery). Returning to Ireland in the 5th century, Patrick arrived in Saul where he preached in a barn (the Irish for barn is sabhal *from which 'Saul' derives). His ministry succeeded in converting the hitherto aggressively chauvinistic local chieftain, Dilchu, who showed his appreciation by giving Patrick the barn as his first church.*

focused mainly, not in the south, but in Ulster. 'I, Patrick,' he wrote, in dog Latin, in his *Confession*, 'a sinner, the simplest of men . . . was taken away into Ireland in captivity.'

Incarcerated for six years 'near the western sea', tradition has it that he tended sheep as a slave on the lonely slopes of Slemish Mountain in County Antrim, having been sold to the unsympathetic Irish chieftain, Milchu. But Patrick, it seems, had little gift for geographical description and so topographical clues in his writings reproduced, faithfully or otherwise, in the 9th century *Book of Armagh*, are few. After a period away – some authorities would have it that he took holy orders in England; others that he studied in Auxerre in France – he was ordered to return to Ireland, presumably on the suspect grounds that he knew the territory, although according to the *Confession* he was simply acting in response to a voice which had called to him in a vision: 'We beg you, holy boy, to come and walk amongst us once again.'

He died at Saul 60 years later having converted most of the north, adopted the druidic chant as St Patrick's breastplate, accommodated pagan ritual dates within his church's calendar and having – in true saintly fashion – resisted demons disguised as blackbirds, banned snakes and adopted the shamrock as the symbol for the Holy Trinity.

Abbeys and friaries followed in his wake, his successors building where the landfall was good and where clean water flowed. St Comgall raised a monastery school at Bangor, baptized a mermaid and sent St Columbanus and St Gall to mainland Europe to preserve Christianity's flickering light during the continent's Dark Ages. St Finnian built an abbey at Newtownards, St Mochaoi another at Nendrum.

But despite the multitude of legends surrounding Patrick, the warriors he faced down, the demons he expelled, we know nothing of his views on chastity, fornication and masturbation, matters so worrying for the churches in Ireland.

There are those historians who will claim the few stones at Saul are all that are left of his church, destroyed, as in all such legends, by the invading Danes. Now the saint stands, remembered in a vast statue high on Slieve Patrick, 'Patrick's Hill'. A cluster of stone structures in a pretty little valley to the south are deemed St Patrick's Wells and curative properties are claimed for their waters which still spill, like some primitive shower device, in one of the enclosures now referred to as 'the women's baths'.

When Patrick came to the area he would have seen what are still Downpatrick's two dominant hills, each topped with a fort, referred to in common parlance as a 'dun'. On one he built a church thus giving to later generations the name, Dun Patrick.

Of course a dead saint is as useful as a live one, and somewhat less troublesome. So when the Anglo-Norman colonizing forces came north under the command of the self-styled 'Prince of Ulster', John de Courcy, they were just as pragmatic as the good saint had been before them. Alfreca, de Courcy's wife, wishing to create an administrative focus to which dissidents must attend – and so be kept under supervision – decreed that Patrick's remains had been discovered buried at Downpatrick, thus securing the town's status. Such appealing myths have acquired great potency over the centuries as the massive boulder-like gravestone, inscribed 'Patric'(*sic*), but dating from only 1900, attests.

Above: Inch Abbey in Downpatrick. Having conquered much of Ulster in the 12th century, John de Courcy attempted to reduce the power of the existing clergy by replacing Downpatrick's canons with Benedictines and Cistercians. These he housed in elegant new buildings in what are still the tranquil settings of Grey and Inch abbeys.

81

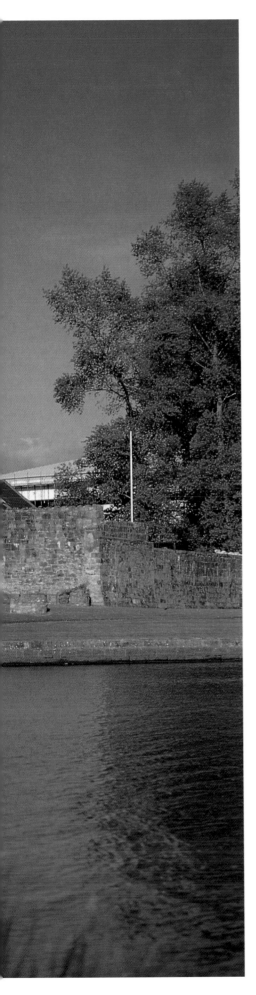

FERMANAGH

A diet of stones and fishes

Mossy headstones in the graveyard on the island of Galloon in the western part of the county of Fermanagh strike notes which resonate across time. On many, a skilled mason of the 18th century has carved, with great craft, those symbols of death which said so much to the people of his time. Here, among the coarse, wet and fresh cut grass, are the cold icons of man's mortality: crossed bones, sand-timer hourglass, bell, coffin and skull.

Yet, it is not the bell tolling the inexorable passing of the hours – recorded by the falling grains of sand – nor the sombre closed-for-ever coffin lids, nor the piratical crossed bones, but rather it is the carved skulls which evoke times before the dawn of Ireland's written history. For they echo the carvings of a cult from the core of Celtic mysticism which can trace its lineage down the centuries in the enigmatic stone heads found scattered across the multitude of islands in this quiet county of reedy lakes, and of fish, and of time standing still.

Major-General, the Honourable Sir Galbraith Lowry Cole, scion of the Cole family who came to the county of Fermanagh in the 1600s, also looks down in stone effigy, cavalry sabre in hand, over the four hills of Enniskillen, the island county town. Were the sabre a telescope, he could scan the 50 watery miles (80 km) of the two Loughs Erne which dominate Fermanagh, fed by the River Erne which winds its way north and west from its bubbling County Cavan source to where it enters the sea among Donegal's surf beaches.

At the general's stone feet, as it were, is Enniskillen. Its one long main street curls east to west, traversing four hills, two bridges and changing its name a handful of times as it does. The hills offer an encapsulation of its strengths. On the farthest, Portora Royal School traces its origins back to 1608 and the Plantation – the playwrights Oscar Wilde and Samuel

Left: Enniskillen Castle, in origin a stronghold built by local Irish chieftains in the early 15th century, was rebuilt by William Cole in the early 17th century.

Beckett, are among its alumni. On the next are the Anglican Cathedral of St MacCartin's, Catholic St Michael's and the Wesleyan Chapel. The next is the Townhall's hill. The fourth hill, Fort Hill, is the general's.

At its foot, by the East Bridge, stands the Cenotaph, where, at 11.00 a.m. each Remembrance Sunday in early November, old men with burnished medals, Boy Scouts with shining shoes and nurses in uniform, gather in silence to remember friends, fathers, grandfathers and great-grandfathers (of all religions and of no religion) who gave their lives during the two world wars. At the 1987 Remembrance Day service the IRA detonated a bomb among those so gathered, killing 11 and shattering the bodies of many more.

No other killing so moved Ireland. War-hardened reporters, who had seen it all, could not fight back tears. President Reagan and Charles Haughey, the Republic of Ireland's *Taoiseach* (Prime Minister), spoke of their revulsion, the Pope of his shock. On stage, in concert in America, Bono, of the Dublin group U2, cursed Irish-Americans who fund the terrorists.

There is a new Cenotaph now, and dotted along the rows of solid Georgian merchants' houses which flank this main street, are the Convent School, the Orangemen's Hall, the Court House, the Presbyterian Church, the two local newspaper offices, a scattering of bistros, gift shops and a dozen atmospheric pubs made cosmopolitan with the accents of Dutch, French, German and Swiss who have cruised and fished the great lakes as holidaymakers, undeterred, even through the worst of the 'Troubles', letting the county know its future is tourism.

'Cole's Pole', as the Enniskillen people term the pillar on which the general's statue stands, is fluted and Doric. Over the centuries the Coles, who became the Earls of Enniskillen, came, both directly, and by intermarriage with Planter and Gaelic families, to control every rolling arable acre, every lakeside castle – Archdale, Caldwell, Coole, Crevenish, Crom, Hume, Magrath, Maguire, Monea, Portora, Saunderson and Tully – and even policed the lakes through the 17th and 18th centuries. The family ran the county as a private fiefdom. Thirteen of them were members of the British Parliament in the period 1661–1885.

Socially they were as other Anglo-Irish families. They employed professionals to sail their yachts, engaged governesses to teach their daughters French, had their sons tutored to serve as high sheriffs at home, and as generals abroad. They vied with their neighbours as to who could build the finest house and sculpt nature to its most ordered. Thus

Right: Once plentiful in Lough Erne the pike was given the death-blow by unregulated overfishing during the 'Troubles'. However, while the old commercial freshwater fishing industries have all but disappeared – the pollan, victims to pollution, and the eels to a lack of young men wishing to follow a life wrought hard in chilling early morning mists – the lough is well-stocked with what are dismissively termed 'coarse' or 'white' fish: bream and roach and the delightful, predatory perch, as well as ever increasing numbers of both trout and salmon.

Left: The Janus Figure, one of a pair of impressive stone figures which stand among the bracken in the graveyard on the island of Bon. Each one is made up of two busts set back to back, carved on a single stone – one face looking back to the old year, the other looking forward to the new. Their expressions are blank. One mouth is an open slit; in another the tongue shows, teeth bared. Chins are pointed, hair plaited; a belt suggests uniform and rank. There are crossed limbs, legs akimbo. One figure is male, aroused. No one knows precisely from which century they date, although archaeologists and anthropologists speak of blood sacrifice and rites of fertility.

Fermanagh's inheritance from the Coles includes: Castle Coole, Ireland's finest Palladian mansion; Florence Court, a more modest Georgian concoction; battle honours for Enniskillen's Cathedral and misty photographs of aged yachts, so beloved of coffee-table book editors.

There, an interest in the family might have ceased had they not dabbled in scientific pursuits natural to the area. The name of Lady Dorothy Galbraith Cole is still associated with her work in recording the county's cult. For the Celts of the 3rd century BC, the carved human head was the house of the spirit, and just as the cross is the icon of the Christian, so decapitation, not crucifixion, figures in Celtic myth.

Carved heads are found on the ruined churches and crosses scattered liberally by the lakes, none more fascinating than the six half-pagan, half-Christian images cemented into the tiny 12th-century, ruined church on White Island. The first figure on the left is a squatting female – grotesque – cheeks bulging; mouth grinning; legs wide apart. She is aroused, bestriding the bridge from pagan exultation and Christian disapproval. Such figures are termed *Sheela na Gigs* and their presence in holy Ireland has given many a god-fearing archaeologist hours of soul-searching.

The Coles' other scientific diversion was fish. Quite rightly so, for the Erne and its catchment has much to reveal. There are big trout to troll for on the Lower Lough Erne and plenty of smaller ones to take the mayfly. Salmon, almost destroyed by the hydro-electric barrier at Ballyshannon, are effecting a return.

There is also the delightful charr – olive black, pink-spotted – a distant relative of the salmon, left behind in a scattering of Irish loughs when the ice age retreated. The many sub-species of charr swimming in Ireland's isolated lakes are mostly named after those who first recorded them for scientific journals. In Lough Eske is found Cole's charr, named for the 3rd Earl of Enniskillen, whose donation of the first specimen in the 1860s was but one of his many contributions, for which the British Museum is no doubt eternally grateful.

MONAGHAN

Lost for words

WHEREAS THE COUNTY of Cavan – its surface dimpled with little hollows filled with water – had its name Anglicized from the descriptive Irish for 'the hollow place', *An Cabhan*, County Monaghan takes its Anglicized title from the equally appropriate Irish, *Muineachan*, 'the place of little thicketed hills'. However, despite the wild beauty of its scenery and the neat geometry of its Planters' and English garrison towns with their slim-spired Gothic churches and stout Georgian houses, this county has tended to receive a bad press from its many native authors.

While rough woodland and vanilla-scented gorse spreads over the poor soil of humpy hills, the water – and there is water everywhere – drains down over the boggy ground into little reed-fringed lakes whose shores are often too sodden to approach with any degree of safety.

Once this was a good place to hide, if you were desperate enough. First, Stone Age peoples, and later the early Christians, retreated here from their invaders, who contented themselves, in the main, with the richer lands east and west which offered easier pickings with less likelihood of ambush. The Vikings and the Normans kept to the plains of Louth, leaving only small bands of marauders supporting the Irish chiefs who operated hit-and-run forays from the damp chill of Monaghan's mist-shrouded hollows. Even when Oliver Cromwell invaded in 1649, his massacres of the Catholic Irish were kept mainly to the coast, though his subsequent mass deportations were not.

Throughout the 17th century, the Planters, mostly from Scotland, took only the best land, clearing it to grow flax and raise sheep, and, if they prospered, gentrifying it with meadows and copses of beech, lime, sycamore and chestnut imported to decorate a valley's sweep or a hill's profile. In Monaghan's villages, as in those of eastern Antrim, the Scots Ulster tongue, with its Scottish pronunciations, its economy of put-down

Left: Sometimes undulating, sometimes hussocky, the landscape of Monaghan is made up of hundreds of teardrop-shaped drumlin hills.

and its directness of humour, survives in the language of the fair day, the corner shop counter and the harvest.

But the land around Inniskeen, *Inis Caoin,* 'the pleasant island' on the little River Fane, is now comprehensively signposted as 'Kavanagh Country', as rural tourism searches for its niche to market. Here, the harsh lives of its poor farmers working the 'black hills' were immortalized by that irascible, embittered, cruelly critical, but wonderful poet, Patrick Kavanagh (1904–67):

> *My black hills have never seen the sun rising,*
> *Eternally they look north towards Armagh.*
> *Lot's wife would not be salt if she had been*
> *Incurious as my black hills that are happy*
> *When dawn whitens Glassdrummond chapel.*

Above : Patrick Kavanagh (sculpture by John Coll) admires the view on the banks of Dublin's Grand Canal.

FROM: 'SHANCODUFF' BY PATRICK KAVANAGH

Below: Inniskeen, where Kavanagh was born and lived until he was 35 years old.

Kavanagh was born the son of a subsistence farmer who supplemented his income by cobbling. The poems he wrote were linked closely to the landmarks around his home. 'Inniskeen' and 'Shancoduff' are among his most affectionate. While such works as his autobiography, *The Green Fool,* and his *roman à clef, Tarry Flynn,* celebrate the charms and delights

of his bucolic upbringing, they also rigorously condemn the crass absurdities of rural poverty. His major work, *The Great Hunger*, is decidedly anti-pastoral and never won favour with any establishment; his grimmer visions of the poor farmer's life running contrary to the idyllic conventions of the Irish literary revival. In short, Kavanagh opposed art as nationalism, heritage as future and the rosy-tinted view of a mystical, mythical landscape, and in Dublin his cantankerous nature and his unflinchingly savage criticism of fellow writers left him with few friends.

John McGahern is another writer to come from the poor farmlands of south Ulster. The son of a police sergeant, he grew up in Cootehill on the Monaghan–Cavan border in the late 1930s and his grim tales tell of harsh, uncommunicative and introspective local family life, wrought hard under an incessant rain.

His first novel, *The Barracks*, was published to critical acclaim in 1963. Two years later his second, *The Dark*, was banned under the Republic's Church-inspired 1929 Censorship of Publications Act and also cost him his job as a teacher. The unspoken emotions he dissects expose a repressive world of ordinary people from both sides in the civil war of 1922: of policemen, nurses and teachers; of ancient hatreds passed down from generation to generation, submerged in the Irish *omertàs* which make taboo so many aspects of tenderness and sexual expression; of the fear and secrecy surrounding the country's age-old political vendettas.

Following the banning of *The Dark*, McGahern was forced to leave Ireland for a time. Now returned, his acute and painful presentation of the dark, closed side of rural Ireland have brought him respect, but no popular affection.

Monaghan's metropolises: Ballybay, Bailieborough, Castleblaney, Carickmacross and Clones all run to the pattern of south Ulster Plantation towns, with the wide main street, the crisp spire of the Planters' Gothic Church, the stern court house, the solid market house, the charming almshouse, the castle, the tumbled abbey, the Norman ruin, the drumlin hill and the little lake.

Some towns are bright as new pins, prosperous from new light industries; others reek of neglect. Here, wind blows chip papers across main squares – 'diamonds' in the local parlance – past pollution-blackened high crosses whose carved depictions of Adam and Eve are almost undistinguishable amid the grime and street detritus. Old paint bubbles, and cracks cover the once-fine Georgian window-sills, protected here and there by cast-iron spikes, originally designed to deter fair day cattle, or their roistering herders keen on a sit-down after a pint or two. Street names are often the last memorials to the town's long-departed founding fathers.

Visiting the county town of Monaghan itself must have made a lasting impression on the enquiring minds of boys and girls growing up on farms and in tiny villages. Its history would, no doubt, have been drummed into them at their school desks. They would have been told that it traces its past back to the Crannog – a man-made island – in the lake in the grounds of St Louis Convent which was used by the local chieftains as their 14th-century base.

Today, the town's pride rests on other things, such as its new theatre, The Garage. Here, many of Ireland's more adventurous touring theatrical companies, from north and south of the border, carry on the island's long tradition of 'fit ups' – whereby actor-managers brought the classics, farce and melodrama to the stages of even the smallest towns – as well as celebrating, to good effect, the sometimes uncomfortable truths contained in the works of the wetland writers.

Above: Named for their call which sounds like two stones being tapped together, stonechats, found throughout Ireland, are typically seen, as here, perched on the top of Monaghan's many gorse bushes.

TYRONE

From here to the White House

THIS IS A WILD COUNTY where buzzards swoop over empty moors and the genetic skeins of so many US presidents and frontiersmen were knitted together. Woodrow Wilson's family still farm land at Dergalt on the Plumbridge Road outside Strabane. Whitewashed and thatched over its oak roof timbers, the old house is furnished as it should be: a dresser stands on the clay floor; a kettle sings in the hearth; a portrait of Judge James, Woodrow's grandfather, hangs above it. Wilson's grandmother, Annie Adams, came from Sion Mills, a few miles further south. She met James in 1807 on an emigrant ship sailing west from Ulster for the Americas. They had ten children of whom the tenth was Woodrow Wilson's father, Joseph.

Five Ulstermen had signed the Declaration of American Independence in 1776 and, indeed, much of what was written in the declaration can be traced back to the writings of another Ulster-Scot, one who never made the tortuous voyage west. The philosopher, Francis Hutcheson, who died 40 years before, had written extensively on rights which were unalienable, on liberty and on the pursuit of happiness.

No surprise then that, in all, over a dozen Ulstermen – descendants of those who made up this second wave – made it to the White House: Susanna Boylston Adams, mother of John Adams, the second president (1797–1801), came from Ulster-Scots farmers; the fifth president (1817–25), James Monroe, took his family name from Mount Roe, just across the Tyrone border, in Derry; while the sixth president (1825–29) was John Quincy Adams, son of John Adams.

Andrew Jackson, the seventh president (1829–37), claimed to have been born in 1767 on an emigrant ship on the high seas. He led the fight against the English at the Battle of New Orleans. The grandfather of Andrew Johnson, the seventeenth president (1865–69), emigrated from

Left: In an area of rich prehistoric remains, Beaghmore's stone circles are thought to have been laid out in the manner of an ancient fertility rite.

the tiny village of Ballyclare – which also claims Mark Twain's family roots – in 1750. Chester Alan Arthur, the twenty-first president (1881–85), was, like Jackson and Buchanan, a first generation American. His father William left Dreen, Cullybackey, in 1816. Grover Cleveland, the twenty-second and twenty-fourth president (1885–89 and 1893–97), owes his Scots-Irish ancestry to his maternal grandfather, Abner Neal, a bookseller who left Ulster late in the 18th century.

Benjamin Harrison, the twenty-third president (1889–93), had two great, great, grandparents of Ulster descent. The family of William McKinley, the twenty-fifth president (1897–1901), left Conagher near Ballymena in 1743 and Richard Milhous Nixon, the thirty-seventh president (1969–74), had ancestors who left Ulster in 1853.

Details of all the presidents past and present – President Clinton's people came from Ballycassidy – and of all the presidents' men and women can be found among the displays at the Ulster-American Folk Park at Camphill, near the county town of Omagh, with its unevenly matched double-spired Sacred Heart Church.

Over chauvinistic to some, uncomfortably parochial or too exclusively Protestant in its origins to others, the park nevertheless certainly offers much to the understanding of today's Ulster. Some of the information is amusing; some arcane; some instructive. John Paul Getty's family, we learn, came from Ulster-Scots stock. So did those of Henry 'Billy the Kid' McCarty, James Butler 'Wild Bill' Hickok, William Frederick 'Buffalo Bill' Cody and Robert Leroy Parker, more famous under his alias, 'Butch Cassidy'.

So, too, did the families of three of the earliest astronauts, John Glenn, Neil Armstrong and James B. Irwin, as well as those of Gene Kelly and Marion Mitchell Morrison, the latter better known as John Wayne. The film, *The Searchers*, embodied much of what the Ulster-Scots stood for.

In truth, however, the Sperrin Mountains north and west of Omagh may better serve to place man's efforts in nature's perspective. They emit an eerie air of ominous other-worldliness scarce in the north. But there are

Below: The signing of the Declaration of Independence on 4th July 1776 by John Hancock, Thomas McKeane, James Smith, George Taylor and Matthew Thornton, all Ulster-Scots. A sixth Ulsterman, Charles Thompson, as secretary to the Continental Congress, was the man who wrote it down and gave it its first public reading.

good trout in the bubbling streams which rush under the pretty arched, stone bridges. There is even a little gold panning and the rare (and protected) freshwater mussel which may secrete the even rarer freshwater pearl. What if the clouds scudding behind you over the lonely moor do cast an ominous shadow, hurrying you to the village pub before dusk?

Once densely forested – now speckled with grid-planted forest parks – the county was the last stronghold of the O'Neills and the O'Donnells, earls of Tyrone and Tryconnell, holding out against the English until the flight of the earls in 1607.

Those who stayed behind rebelled in 1641, massacring Scots and English settlers in a killing to be rued in 1649 when Cromwell took revenge at Drogheda, putting the town to the sword. No trace of the true O'Neills is to be found, bar their crowning place on top of a tree-ringed hill at Tullaghoge outside Cookstown.

An even grimmer history surrounds Harry Aimbreidh O'Neill's 500 year-old, twin-towered ruin near Newtownstewart. His sister was grossly disadvantaged – those that spoke of her said she had a head like a pig. But Aimbreidh (pronounced 'Avery') wanted her wed and offered a dowry large enough to attract a flutter of suitors. He also added a sub-clause of Shakespearean subtlety, namely that any suitor to gain the dowry must commit himself to marriage without seeing the girl. A later change of intent would mean not only loss of the dowry, but also of the suitor's life by the hangman's noose.

It is said that such was his sister's affliction and fortune that 19 men were put to the scaffold. Was it for her pleasure? Or his madness? Who can judge him now, not knowing the needs of the 15th century? However, such was his unshakable resolve and determination that a few of his genes must surely have become intertwined with those of the men and women who conquered the American wilderness.

Above: Taken by James Mellon when he visited Camphill in 1874, this unique photograph shows the cottage from where his father, Thomas Mellon, born on 3rd February 1813, emigrated to the United States to become judge, banker and reputedly the richest man of his day. The Mellon Cottage, now restored, forms the core of the Ulster American Folk Park which was set up by one of Thomas Mellon's descendants to tell the story of the many thousands of Ulster Scots who emigrated from Ireland at the beginning of the 19th century . A replica of the Mellon Cottage also stands in Pittsburgh, Pennsylvania.

THE PROVINCE OF
LEINSTER

THE ATLANTIC OCEAN, that vast machine which daily churns out the weather for western Europe, dashes against the shores of three of Ireland's four provinces. Leinster is the exception. Apart from a tiny strip of coastline on the southern slopes of County Wexford, the province is bathed by the milder waters of the Irish Sea, a stretch of water which in comparison is little more than a large lake.

While the Atlantic has carved out massive gashes and has flooded river valleys in the coastlines of Ulster, Connacht and Munster, the Irish Sea coast of Leinster runs in more or less a straight line from north to south.

There is little of the savage grandeur of mountains tumbling into the sea that characterizes the rest of the Irish coastline. In Wicklow there are mountains indeed, but they slope gently towards sandy shores, while elsewhere the sea is bordered by lush, flat pastureland.

Leinster looks east. It is less remote from the rest of Europe and its coastline in earlier times lay open to invaders and immigrants from Britain and the mainland. The Vikings founded many of the coastal towns, the indigenous population being rural rather than urban dwellers. The Normans began their conquest in Leinster, and so, too, did the English who followed them.

Large settlements grew, and for centuries – until the industrial revolution – Dublin, the province's and the country's capital, was the only place on the entire island which could justifiably call itself a city by international standards.

Dublin today is still the largest urban agglomeration, and one person in five in the island of Ireland – one in three in the Republic – lives there. It dominates the country and dominates the province even more.

The extent of this dominance can be shown by some comparisons: if the same population ratio of capital city to country existed, as does that

Left: Despite the concern of Animal Rights groups, Dublin's monthly Smithfield Fair remains a popular forum for the trading of cheap horseflesh.

Above: The satirist Jonathan Swift (1667–1745) was one of Ireland's greatest 18th century writers.

Below: The Battle of the Boyne, 1690, *(engraving by Adriaan Schoonebeek) between England's recently crowned Protestant King, William III, and his ousted Catholic rival, James II. A significant battle, it saw the death of 500 Williamites and 1000 Jacobites.*

between Dublin and the Republic of Ireland, London would have almost 20 million inhabitants; in the United States, Washington would be a city of 100 million; in Germany, Berlin would house 27 million souls; Moscow would harbour 50 million Russians and Beijing would be home to 400 million Chinese.

But the Republic is a very small country, and Dublin, by European standards, is no more than a medium-sized city; only Helsinki and Luxembourg, of the 15 capital cities of the European Union, are smaller in size.

The dominance, however, remains. In Leinster the next largest town, Dundalk, in County Louth, is just one-thirtieth of Dublin's size. There are, of course, historical reasons for this. Ireland's population is now little over half what it was before the Great Famine began in 1845, while the Dublin urban area has grown four-fold in the same period.

Dublin's pre-eminence has not only been in the area of population. In architecture, despite the ravages of time, it outshines all other urban areas; in music, the arts, medicine and science it has produced the leading Irish exponents. In industry, Belfast left Dublin far behind, but the advent of computer technology has given Dublin a boost.

It is, however, in the field of literature that Dublin has made its greatest contribution, not only to Ireland but also to the world. What other city of its size has produced writers of the stature of Jonathan Swift, Sir Richard Steele, Richard Brinsley Sheridan, Oscar Wilde, Bernard Shaw, W. B. Yeats, James Joyce, Samuel Beckett, Sean O'Casey, Brendan Behan and, in the field of political letters, Edmund Burke?

Dublin, despite this, is not Ireland, and neither is it totally representative of Leinster. The great plains of Meath and Westmeath; the vast boglands of Offaly; the mountain fastnesses of Wicklow; the long

stretch of the River Shannon to the west; the unique county of Wexford; the ancient town of Kilkenny, all have attractions of an entirely different nature from the Georgian streets and squares of Dublin.

Leinster has what could be described as two coastlines, that of the Irish Sea to the east and of the Shannon to the west. The sea coast has long stretches of sandy shore from Clogherhead in County Louth all the way to the popular beaches of Wexford and Wicklow. The Shannon is by far the longest river in Ireland. Described by Edmund Spenser as 'the spacious Shenan spreadeing like a sea', it flows from north to south along the shores of Longford, Westmeath and Offaly, bursting forth at one point into the expanse of Lough Ree, where it takes little imagination to consider oneself out of touch with land.

The remains of the ancient monastic settlement of Clonmacnois, founded by St Kieran, borders the river in County Offaly, rivalled only by St Kevin's foundation at Glendalough in County Wicklow.

There are other rivers of importance too. The Barrow and the Nore flow in a southeasterly direction and are navigable in parts. The Boyne runs from east to west reaching the Irish Sea at the ancient town of Drogheda, and few rivers in Ireland run by more historic sites.

The Battle of the Boyne at Oldbridge, near Drogheda, where William III defeated James II, with the British monarchy at stake, changed the whole order of Ireland for centuries. Much earlier the banks of the Boyne were home to prehistoric man, as the burial grounds of Newgrange – older than the pyramids of Egypt – Knowth and Dowth, bear witness.

Leinster offers, uniquely in Ireland, the amenities of a capital city coupled with the quiet pleasures of the countryside, the one accessible to the other in minutes rather than in hours.

Above: The Wicklow Mountains, which are clearly visible from Dublin, provide a stark contrast to the lush valleys and abundant woodlands that surround them. Despite quite extensive forestry plantations, this highland area remains wild and beautiful, much of it dotted with ancient clumps of Scots pine and covered with mile upon mile of rolling heather.

CARLOW

County of the nearly famous

CARLOW IS A SMALL COUNTY, the second smallest in Ireland. Its claims are modest, but its land is productive. It is here that the coastal mountain ranges of the east meet the rich, if featureless, central plain. It was in Carlow, too, that the Normans, following their 12th century arrival in neighbouring Wexford, began to consolidate their conquest; it was here that they built their first castles, thus leaving their mark permanently on the landscape.

The rugged beauty of the Blackstairs Mountains quickly slope to a rich pastureland, watered by the broad and navigable River Barrow which was envied and taken by a succession of invaders who themselves blended with the Celtic inhabitants to produce a population, unpretentious in the main, but with more than its average share of eccentrics.

Like many parts of Ireland, Carlow supplied migrants to the rest of the English-speaking world. But in many cases they were well-to-do, Protestant rather than Roman Catholic, and far from the archetype of the famine-stricken who crowded the cities of Britain and the United States in the 19th century.

Those fortunate enough to own large holdings were prosperous and such people find time to devote their mental energies to matters other than managing their estates. Many, in any event, were wealthy enough to employ professional managers while they got on with their pet, often unconventional, projects.

Others, from the merchant class, in what was, and to a great extent still is, a prosperous corner of Ireland, made enough money to involve themselves in similar activities.

Samuel Haughton was one of the eccentrics who abounded in the Ireland of the Victorian era. Born in Carlow, he was a scientist and mathematician and graduated in mathematics from Trinity College

Left: Carlow, Ireland's second smallest county, is situated in one of the country's most fertile regions.

Above: Leighlinbridge Castle, originally called the Black Castle, was built by the Norman Hugh de Lacy in 1180. The present ruin is all that remains of a later construction by Sir Edward Bellingham in 1547 which fell to Cromwell's forces in 1650. The nine-arched bridge over the River Barrow was completed in 1320 and is said to be the oldest bridge in Ireland.

Dublin before turning his attention to medicine. He is best remembered for a discovery which combined all three disciplines at which he was adept. It took some time to work out, mind you, but in the end his formula was of benefit to a tiny percentage of the population, although it stopped dramatically short of saving their lives.

Haughton worked out a mathematical, scientific and medical computation known as 'Haughton's Drop'. The 'drop' was not one of medicinal liquid but an instruction to the hangman when dealing with prisoners sentenced to death. Until this time, the unfortunate wretches sentenced to be 'hanged by the neck until dead' usually suffered from a slow and agonizing process of strangulation, something which the mob that gathered for executions thoroughly enjoyed.

'Haughton's Drop' took the 'fun' out of execution day. It determined the precise length of rope; the exact depth of fall which a condemned man of a certain weight required in order to die instantly rather than linger half-alive in front of his viewers.

Carlow appears to have had the knack for producing 'once famous sons and daughters', those talented men and women who made well-known contributions to society in their time, but who are now half, or totally, forgotten.

While everyone has heard of Henry Ford, whose ancestors came from County Cork, the name Frederick York Wolseley may not immediately ring a bell or blow a horn. The Wolseleys came from Mount Wolseley in the county and Fred was an ambitious chap who headed off to New South Wales in 1867 where he invented an ingenious device to shear sheep mechanically.

From there he came back to the 'home countries' settling in England where he and Herbert Austin produced the first British automobile, the Wolseley Three-Wheeler. The Wolseley dominated the British auto market for some time and the name was only withdrawn from the market in 1975. Frederick died in London in 1899 and his grave was unmarked

until 1988 when the Australians celebrated their country's bicentenary.

So it is that many Carlow people have made names for themselves both at home and abroad. Patrick Francis Moran, from the quaint village of Leighlinbridge, became Cardinal Archbishop of Sydney where his statue adorns St Mary's Cathedral. John Tyndall, from the same village, was the 19th century scientist who discovered why the sky was blue and then spent most of his life getting as close to it as was possible. He was the first person to climb the Weisshorn in the Swiss Alps and one of the first to climb the Matterhorn.

Tyndall was also a pioneer in the field of fibre optics which play a major part in the communications industry of today. This achievement is commemorated by a monument erected at Alp Lusgen by his distraught and remorseful widow in 1911. Mrs Tyndall had every reason to be unhappy, her unwitting application of an overdose of chloral to her unfortunate 73-year-old husband in 1873 having been the cause of his sad demise.

Others to escape, and I use the word advisedly, from Carlow were Peter Fenelon Collier of Myshall who founded the US publishers of *Collier's Magazine* and William Dargan, Ireland's great railway entrepreneur who made a vast fortune, invested badly and died almost penniless in Dublin in 1867.

The greatest Carlow escape artist of all was Patrick Robert 'Paddy' Reid, who was the British escape officer at the German prisoner-of-war camp in Colditz. As well as engineering many daring escapes from the notorious castle in eastern Germany, Reid managed to make an unscheduled exit himself.

Those sons and daughters of Carlow who stayed at home may have failed to make a name for themselves, but they live in a pleasant place bordered by the Blackstairs Mountains to the east and watered by the great River Barrow. It is one of the few counties in Leinster which does not form a section of Ireland's large but often featureless Central Plain.

Above: Viewed from Mount Leinster, Carlow's vibrant tapestry of lush pasture and rich arable land stretches away as far as the eye can see.

DUBLIN

A splendid city

AT THE BEGINNING of the 17th century the Great Duke Ormonde proclaimed that 'it was of vital importance to keep up the splendour of the government'; that the populace of Dublin, and therefore of Ireland as a whole, should know who was in power and the importance of that power should be impressed upon them. The political motivation behind this statement may have been open to question, but it was from this pragmatic principle that the glories of Dublin's architecture stemmed.

The Phoenix Park with its 1,750 acres (708 ha), the sum of all the public parks in central London put together, was the first project. Next came the Royal Hospital in Kilmainham in 1680. Ormonde vetoed plans which would have seen the great houses of Dublin, like those in many cities and towns in Great Britain and Ireland, turn their backs on the central river and thus be hidden from view. He insisted on the Parisian model: houses should face the water; quays should be built and the 'splendour of the government' displayed.

Ormonde's principle dominated the development of Dublin for more than a century. However, by 1690 the balance of power had swung dramatically towards the 'Protestant Party' with the defeat of the Catholic King James II by King William III at the Boyne, just 30 miles (48 km) north of Dublin. Catholics were debarred from office, high and low, their churches closed and their places of worship confined to small rooms in back alleys.

Unprincipled and undemocratic as the new regime was, it led to a period during which the city's Protestants – and Dublin was largely a Protestant city – became secure enough in themselves to settle more comfortably into Irish life.

In Dublin, a period of stability and self-confidence, not to mention considerable wealth, ensued which soon found its expression in an

Left: Laid out in 1762, Merrion Square exemplifies some of Dublin's most elegant Georgian architecture. Its many famous occupants included W.B. Yeats.

103

Right: A stained glass window in the Royal Hospital in Kilmainham. Built in 1680 and modelled on Les Invalides *in Paris, Dublin's Royal Hospital was the predecessor of the Royal Hospital in Chelsea, London.*

unprecedented expansion of the city. This growth, unlike elsewhere in Europe, took place to the east of the old town rather than to the west.

Development came thick and fast. Great town-houses were built for titled landowners, first north of the River Liffey and later to the south. In 1713 the city decided that there should be a 'Mansion House . . . for the honour and advantage of this city, and a convienency (*sic*) to the Lord Mayor', so a large house, built by Joshua Dawson in 1705, was purchased and extended. It stands today on Dawson Street.

As well as encouraging architectural development, the period of stability began to engender among the Irish Protestant ascendancy a feeling of separateness, even of independence, from their cousins in Britain. It was a phenomenon not dissimilar to the quest for independence from London on the part of the colonists in North America.

By 1729 the first stone of a new Irish Parliament House was laid on College Green. The building was to be an essay in classical elegance, and on a far more monumental scale than the buildings that then housed the Parliament in London which had supremacy over its Irish counterpart. Its colonnades inspired Robert Smirke's design for the British Museum a hundred years later.

The Irish Parliament, scene of many dramatic incidents in later years, voted subventions for the rebuilding of Trinity College across the road and soon the two buildings formed the northern and eastern sides of a stylish plaza.

In 1741 the 'Musick Hall' was opened in Fishamble Street, site of the medieval 'Fish Shambles', and a year later the fame of the burgeoning city in the far west of Europe had spread to the extent that when George Frederick Handel, out of favour with London society, wished to take himself and his music to another capital, it was to Dublin he turned. He had hoped, as his biographer, Mainwaring, wrote in 1760, to 'find that favour and encouragement in a distant capital, which London seemed to refuse him'.

This is precisely what happened, and on 13th April 1742 he gave the first performance of his new oratorio, *Messiah*, at the 'Musick Hall' to an audience of 700 people who were fitted in tightly. Ladies were advised that they should not wear hoops in their skirts, and gentlemen that they should leave their swords at home.

Performed with the help of the choirs of the two Anglican cathedrals, Handel's great work received an ecstatic response with the Revd Dr Patrick Delany so overcome by the performance of 'He was Despised' by Susanna Cibber, that he rose from his seat and exclaimed: 'Woman, for this, be all thy sins forgiven.'

The architectral bonanza continued. Lord Powerscourt built his own town mansion in 1771; Fitzwilliam and Mountjoy squares were laid out in 1791 and Aldborough House, another city mansion for another lord and his family, was opened in 1796. The two most majestic buildings of all, the Custom House and the Four Courts, though north of the Liffey, were constructed right up on the quays to be viewed from the south bank. Confidence abounded, further expansion was expected, but at the height of its growth, events were to take place that would change Dublin from one of Europe's capitals into a provincial town.

Above: The Custom House was built in the late 18th century by James Gandon, the English-born son of a French Huguenot, who was also the architect of the King's Inns.

Below: James Butler, 1st Duke of Ormonde (1610–1688) was a Protestant who, having gone into exile with Charles II, enjoyed the king's favour following the Restoration.

Left: Looking south over Dublin from the Guinness Brewery in St James's Gate which covers 64 acres (26 ha) south of the River Liffey. First established in 1759, this brewery's silky, dark beer, topped with its distinctive, creamy foam remains as popular as ever. To meet the demand, four million pints are produced every day and more beer is exported from here than from any other brewery in Europe. According to statistics from the European Union, the growth in Dublin's economy, generally, is the highest of any city in the Union's 15-country membership and is likely to continue as such for the next decade.

THERE'S
MORE
TO IT
THAN
MEETS
THE
EYE

Left: Dublin's port was first built by the Vikings in the 9th century. Today about 5000 ships and 11 million tonnes of cargo pass through it each year.

The insurrection of 1798 in counties Antrim, Down, Wexford and Mayo, put an end to stability. Plans were laid for the Union of Great Britain and Ireland. The Irish parliament voted for its own dissolution in a welter of bribery and corruption. Dublin society, for all the grandeur of the architecture, the literature and the music, had become thoroughly debauched. 'Men of quality' surrounded themselves with rogues and thugs; claret was consumed in such vast quantities as to astound visitors from abroad; great estates were gambled away; favours were bought and sold, and eventually, the parliament itself was sold to London for money, land and titles.

The chief architect of Union in Ireland was Lord Clare, known to Dubliners as 'Black Jack FitzGibbon'. He was given a final accolade by the populace when they pelted his coffin with dead cats as his funeral procession passed through the city.

Dublin's decline was almost instantaneous. The aristocracy, who had built their town-houses to attend the House of Lords, and the landed gentry who had constructed similar mansions to attend the Commons, had no reason to maintain premises in Dublin. The Georgian buildings with their magnificent fan-lit doors fell, first, into the hands of professional men, the lawyers and doctors, then to unscrupulous slum landlords, and then to decay.

By the start of the 20th century, living conditions in Dublin were among the worst in Europe. The child mortality rate was reported to be higher than in Calcutta. Large families crowded into single rooms of tenements which had once been mansions. Magnificent plasterwork and stucco Cupids, Venuses and Apollos gazed down on scenes of indescribable squalor.

Dublin had once again reached an abysmally low point in its long history of ups and downs. It had thrived as a Viking trading centre. In the early Middle Ages it already had two cathedrals, one within and another outside the city walls. It had been fought over continuously and by the time of Ormonde's arrival, its fortunes had hit the bottom of a trough following half a century of conflict throughout Ireland. But it always had the resilience to rise from the depths.

The impoverishment of the city following the Union in 1800 left the great public buildings intact, but the private mansions suffered. Later, in the struggle for independence and the civil war which followed in the 1920s, the Four Courts and the Custom House were badly damaged in the fighting, but decently restored by the government of the new Irish Free State, perhaps due to a subconscious memory of Ormonde's dictum.

But things got worse before they began to get better. In the second half of the 20th century, many great houses fell to a misguided prosperity rather than to poverty as previously had been the case. Property developers knocked down elegant buildings to replace them with glass-and-concrete structures. The people protested, at first without being listened to. There was a residue of bitterness in the hearts of some people, including those in government, who saw the splendid houses as reminders of former British occupation. However, gradually this has been overcome, but only gradually.

Now, at the close of the century, a construction boom, the likes of which has not been seen since Georgian times is under way. The city is looking to the future with as much confidence as it did more than 200 years ago, but this time with a cautious eye on its heritage as well.

KILDARE

County of the horse

AFTER NEWBRIDGE, on the main road from Dublin to the south, pasture and parkland suddenly disappear to be replaced by a high treeless plain dotted with gorse bushes. This is The Curragh, and if you are early enough on the road, you are likely to see strings of thoroughbred racehorses undergoing their daily exercise.

At any time of day, mist and rain permitting, the starting gates and the large grandstand of Ireland's leading racecourse can be seen. This is the centre of the country's great bloodstock industry with its training establishments – meticulously-kept stud farms owned by some of the richest families on earth – and in the village of Kill, the auction ring of Goff's Bloodstock Sales.

I have sat by that ring and watched spindly-legged yearlings, colts and fillies, make their way shakily round as the auctioneer spies a raised finger and in modulated English public school tones announces the process of the bidding in guineas, not pounds.

The guinea represented one pound and one shilling in earlier times; now it means one pound and five pence. It remained the fictitious unit of currency at Goff's long after decimalization.

Traditions die hard in the bloodstock world. After all, its very basis is in lines of breeding which stretch back to three imported stallions from the east: the Brierley Turk, the Godolphin Arabian and the Darley Arabian. From this trio all thoroughbreds are descended, so every little yearling to stagger its way round Goff's ring is likely to be related at some stage in its ancestry.

In the not so distant past, the stud farms and the bidding at Goff's came from the old Anglo-Irish ascendancy: the county magnates; the great landowners; and the more astute judges of horses from the lower ranks of the 'nobility and gentry of Ireland'. This has now changed. The big

Left: Early morning near The Curragh racecourse where many of the world's top racing thoroughbreds are bred and trained.

Right: A horse being auctioned at Goff's Bloodstock Sales, so named after Robert J. Goff of Newbridge, County Kildare, who was appointed official auctioneer to the Irish Turf Club in 1866. In the mid-1970s Goff's relocated from the Royal Dublin Society's sales paddocks in Dublin to a new site at Kill in County Kildare. Since then the company has expanded considerably. By the end of 1981 they had offered over 50 per cent of the Irish horses sold at public auction in the United Kingdom and Republic of Ireland. In 1993 they sold the most expensive yearling in the world at 1.5 million guineas.

bidders' blood lines nowadays can be as eastern as those of the horses put up for sale. Sheikh Mohammed al Maktoum of Dubai has raised his finger at Goff's to bid in millions of guineas. A line of Their Serene Highnesses, The Aga Khan, have also had strong connections with Irish bloodstock over the years.

The old horsey families of Kentucky and the racing men and women of Britain, France and Italy are represented too, and for those who do not arrive by private helicopter from Dublin airport, there is a large car park to house the Rolls Royces, Bentleys, Mercedes and Porsches of the lesser fry. The bloodstock business is centred on very serious money.

It was always a bit like that, even in Irish legend when The Curragh was reputedly a place for chariot racing and the ancient Brehon Laws listed a complicated set of rules and regulations for the practice of the sport by young men of noble birth.

But racing as we know it today began in Kildare in more modern times, and by 1727, when *Cheney's Racing Calendar* was published for the first time, The Curragh had already become the headquarters of the 'Sport of Kings' in Ireland.

Early on, the great contests were in the form of 'match races' in which one great champion was pitted directly against another. In a contest of this type in September 1751, a steed called Black and All Black took on a rival named Bajazet for a prize of 1,000 guineas. The side bets came to a total of 10,000 guineas, a vast fortune in those times.

By 1812 a new phenomenon arrived on the scene in the form of Patrick Connolly who set up as a 'public trainer' of racehorses at Waterford Lodge. Up to then the landed proprietors trained their own champions, but Connolly and his successors have taken over and the famous training establishments of Kildare and other counties further afield, now dominate the racing industry.

Then came the railways, which made The Curragh easily accessible to the metropolis in Dublin less than 30 miles (48 km) away. When the first Irish Derby was run in 1866, a 'racing special', 30 carriages long, set out from the then Kingsbridge (now Heuston) Station in Dublin bearing the well-to-do, and perhaps some of the ill-intentioned of the capital, to their day's outing of sport.

On that first Derby Day the band of the Third Buffs Regiment was on hand to play martial airs for the ladies and gentlemen, but there was an audible sigh of disappointment when only three runners turned up for a sweepstake of five sovereigns each. The first Irish Derby winner was an

Englishman, James Cockin of Staffordshire, whose horse, Selim, ridden by a jockey with the propitious title of 'Lucky' Maidment, won by eight lengths.

Cockin won again the following year with Golden Plover, again with Maidment as jockey, and this led to unsuccessful attempts of a less than sporting nature to limit the race to horses owned and trained in Ireland.

Even the dark days of civil war in Ireland failed to dim the glory of Derby Day on The Curragh. In 1922, when the country was riven by a conflict between those who supported the treaty which established the new Irish Free State and those who were intransigent in their republicanism, the Derby was held in calm and quiet. The race, with its prize of £4,715, was won by Spike Island, owned by Major Giles Loder, who, it was noted, represented a class which at that time preferred neither the Free State nor the Republic, but a maintenance of the Union with Great Britain.

The Derby was later sponsored by the old Irish Sweeps Trust and by the Anheuser-Busch brewing company of St Louis in the United States, raising the prize money to astronomical levels and attracting further private helicopters to The Curragh in June every year to augment the ordinary racegoers who flock there from all parts of Ireland and abroad.

County Kildare was also the scene of a unique kidnapping in 1983 when the former Derby winner, Shergar, was abducted from the stud of his owner, The Aga Khan, and has never been recovered, despite offers of vast rewards by His Serene Highness.

But horseracing in Ireland and in Kildare is not confined to the super rich. The classics on the flat may be the domain of the wealthy, but racing over jumps, or National Hunt Racing, as it is formally known, is a far more egalitarian sport, with small farmers testing their horses, often successfully, against wealthier opponents.

Not surprisingly in a county where the horse is king, there are a number of large country houses of the old Anglo-Irish ascendancy who spent a great deal of time hunting and racing. One anonymous lady was described by the satirical writer Brian O'Nolan (alias Flann O'Brien and Myles na Gopaleen) as being 'not in the least bit self-conscious when off a horse'.

Below: The 1962 Irish Sweeps Derby – the first to be sponsored by the Irish Sweeps Trust – ended in a photo finish with the French horse Tambourine, ridden by R. Poincelek, named as the winner. In 1986 sponsorship of the Derby was taken over by the current sponsors Budweiser, since when it has been called the Budweiser Irish Derby.

KILKENNY

City of medieval charms

INLAND TOWNS IN IRELAND are, in the main, 18th-century creations, the work of 'improving landlords', their houses being of Georgian vintage with their backs turned to the river on which they were founded. Kilkenny is different. True, like other Irish urban foundations, Dublin excepted, it shuns its great river, the Nore, but here the similarity ends.

Kilkenny is, in essence a medieval town, with a great castle, a magnificent cathedral, some well-preserved merchants houses and a sprinkling of abbeys, churches and inns from the Norman period. By size it is a market town, by ancient charter, and from its cathedral status, it is a city.

Its location made it a convenient place for the holding of parliaments, and one of these, in 1336, introduced the 'Statutes of Kilkenny', an early form of 'apartheid' which aimed to separate the Irish from the Normans. Intermarriage was forbidden, so too was the use of Irish surnames and dress. Clerics and monks of Irish origin were refused admittance to churches and monasteries under Norman control. The ancient Irish game of hurling was expressly prohibited.

These Draconian measures were taken because of fears that the Norman colonists were becoming overly Hibernicized in dress and tongue and recreational habits. However, by the time the statutes were introduced the process of assimilation had advanced to such a stage that most of the Norman inhabitants had Irish blood and many of the Irish were part-Norman. In short, it had become almost impossible to distinguish between one race and the other.

The futility of this attempt at racial separation is most apparent today when one sees young men and boys walking through the city's medieval streets with their hurleys tucked under their arms. In Kilkenny, a county which has won the All-Ireland Hurling Championship more than 20

Left: Built in the 12th century by William the Marshall, Kilkenny Castle became the home of the earls of Ormonde in 1392, remaining so until 1967.

times, the game has acquired an almost religious fervour among its players and supporters.

The failure of the statutes has produced in Kilkenny a unique cross-fertilization between old Irish and Norman which is epitomized in the city itself, a place in which more medieval architecture and lore is compressed into such a small area than in any other town in Ireland.

Kilkenny's heyday came in the six-year span in which it proclaimed itself the capital of Ireland under the 'Confederation of Kilkenny' from 1642 to 1648, when the Roman Catholics, of Irish and Anglo-Irish origin, united briefly and held court with the Papal-Nuncio, Cardinal Rinuccini. But the experiment, bedevilled by rivalries between the two ethnic groups, came to an end with the triumph of the Cromwellians in England and the execution of Charles I. Two years later Cromwell himself arrived and took control after four major assaults over five days.

Built in 1172, Kilkenny Castle has been altered significantly since its original construction by Strongbow, the first Norman conqueror of Ireland. On his death, his nephew, William the Marshall, replaced the original structure with a stone fortress. The Butlers, one of whom had been made Chief Butler of Ireland, took over the castle in 1391, from which time Kilkenny became an Anglo-Irish town with its original inhabitants clustered around St Canice's Cathedral in a small area which is still known today as Irishtown. For the next six centuries, the Butlers, who later became the earls of Ormonde, kept their eye on their lands by establishing Catholic and Protestant branches. If the regime in London favoured Protestant ownership, there were Protestant Butlers to fit the bill; if, as it did on occasions, Catholic ownership found favour, there

Above: Known as 'The Long Cantwell' this effigy dates from about 1320 and is thought to be the lid of the burial chamber of Thomas Cantwell, the head of the Anglo-Norman Cantwell family who were local landowners around the town of Kilfane, where this effigy now stands.

Right: St Canice's Cathedral was built in the 13th century on the site of a monastic settlement founded in the 6th century. Today, all that remains of the monastery is the tall Irish round tower. Contained within the cathedral are a number of sepulchral monuments, carved out of black marble in memory of members of the Butler family, dating back to the Middle Ages.

were Catholic Butlers on hand to take over. The castle and some of the grounds were finally handed over to the Irish state by the 6th Marquess of Ormonde in 1967.

At the bottom of the gently sloping hill from the castle, the old city begins at Shee's Almshouse, which was built in the quaintly named Rose Inn Street in 1588 by Sir Richard Shee and his wife as an institution for the relief of the poor in the town. Nearby in St Mary's Lane is the 13th century church of St Mary and, close at hand, St Kieran's Lane which is famous for its inns and hostelries. The 'Slips', a collection of narrow alleyways which run up from St Kieran's to High Street, were the principal thoroughfares of the medieval town. Today, their modern shopfronts mask many much older façades.

Close to 'The Ring', once a centre of medieval bull baiting, stand the remains of the Franciscan Friary, built in 1232, where Friar John Clyn was an annalist in 1348 and 1349 when the Black Death devastated the city and disease hung in the air like an avenging angel. Friar Clyn's annals end as follows: 'I leave parchment to carry out the work if perchance any man survives . . .' After that entry, the annals continue in a different hand. The Friary now stands in the grounds of Smithwick's Brewery, a Guinness subsidiary, whose Kilkenny Beer sells in 'Irish' pubs from Moscow to Milan.

Towering over the town, is the magnificent St Canice's Cathedral which was built by Bishop de Mappleton in 1251–56. The second largest medieval church in Ireland – after St Patrick's Cathedral in Dublin – St Canice's stands on the site of an ancient monastic settlement founded by St Cainneach (anglicized as Canice or Kenny) the only remnant of which is its 100 foot (30.5 m) round tower. During Cromwell's brief stay in Kilkenny, in 1650, he left his iconoclastic mark on the cathedral, destroying the 'idols' and using the nave as a stable for his horses.

Just to the south is Kilkenny College or 'the Grammar School', built by the 1st Duke of Ormonde in 1666. Among its early alumni are several famous men. One was Jonathan Swift, the great satirist and later Dean of St Patrick's in Dublin; another was the poet and playright William Congreve. George Berkeley, the philosopher and Bishop of Cloyne, who gave his name to the university city of Berkeley in California, was a third. One cannot help feeling that the unique city in which they received their secondary education, before moving to Trinity College, Dublin and onwards, must have played a part in developing their imaginations and preparing them for the careers which brought them international renown.

Left: Kilkenny city is home to approximately 52 pubs of which the Marble City Bar, established in 1709, is one of the oldest. It is also one of the best known, having appeared on numerous postcards over the years.

LAOIS

A French refuge

THE TOWN OF Portarlington, which lies on a bend in the River Barrow not far from the border with the county of Offaly, is now a quiet backwater of County Laois. Once it was the scene of a remarkable demographic experiment which made it a place unique in Ireland; a place in which a language was spoken, a religion practised, and a culture installed, which was totally distinct from the surrounding region.

Following the revocation in 1685 of the Edict of Nantes, which had ensured religious tolerance, French Protestant refugees flocked to what was then the United Kingdom of Great Britain and Ireland in search of places in which they could live in peace. One of the many places they settled was Portarlington, and nowhere did their culture, religion and language survive more tenaciously.

Why did the separate identity remain intact for so long? There are many theories put forward. First, Portarlington was surrounded by bogs and forest and therefore sufficiently isolated from the rest of the countryside to maintain a separate identity. Second, the settlement was large enough to be self-sufficient and third, the place had a distinctive character in that an astonishingly high proportion of its families were of noble origin.

The establishment of the French communities took place at a time when, in another Irish paradox, Roman Catholic Irish soldiers were fleeing to France after the Jacobite defeat at the hands of King William III, and it was one of William's senior lieutenants, the Huguenot Henri Massue, Marquis de Ruvigny, later styled Earl of Galway, who got the Portarlington project under way.

Portarlington had been laid out for English settlers with a market square and four streets leading from it. But the little town had suffered severe damage during the war, and de Ruvigny personally financed the

Left: Timahoe Round Tower, seen here in the distance, is the only remnant of the early monastery founded by St Mochua.

Right: Morrissey's bar and grocery was founded by E.J. Morrissey in 1775. Almost all the old furnishings remain. In 1876 an additional storey was added to the house and according to the manager, John Lanigan, this was the last time the place was touched. 'Everything in the bar is the same as it was originally... everything that is except the staff.'

construction of over 100 houses of unique design. The entrances and gardens were to the rear and blank walls faced the streets.

The first wave of immigrants arrived in 1692, many of whom were pensioned-off soldiers and their families. Most came from the officer class, which, at that time, was made up of sons of noble families. There were six ensigns, one cornet, 16 lieutenants, 12 captains and one lieutenant-colonel. The most elegant and magnificent of all, with his scarlet cloak and silver-buckled breeches, was Robert d'Ully, Vicomte de Laval, a man of the royal blood line of King Henri de Navarre.

However, the nobles of that era could hardly have been expected to fend for themselves, and a second group of *laboureurs*, 13 families in all, arrived from the Swiss cantons where they had taken refuge, and gave the colony a more balanced character.

So by the start of the 18th century the foundations of a lasting settlement were laid. There were stories from visitors from neighbouring areas of noblemen sipping a strange drink called tea from tiny china cups under trees in the village square; of the wine of Bordeaux being favoured over the whiskey of the surrounding countryside.

Very soon, however, a number of forces combined to change the situation. The French Calvinists had initially been given freedom from interference by the episcopacy of the established Anglican Church of Ireland. But the arrival of a high-church bishop, William Moreton, from England changed all that. Exceptionally tolerant (for a man of his time) of the Roman Catholic majority in his diocese, he had an abhorrence of Protestant dissenters and was determined to enforce Anglican conformity on the French enclave.

The minister at the *Eglise Française de St Paul*, Revd Benjamin de Daillon, practised a very strict Calvinistic form of worship which was by no means to the bishop's liking. Daillon was replaced in 1702 by a former army chaplain, Antoine Ligenier de Bonneval, who had already embraced Anglicanism and thus began a schism, a major split in the community, which lasted for 26 years.

The turning point came when 37 families left for Dublin to worship at the French Calvinist churches in the capital, where their distinct language and customs were overwhelmed in a city which was quickly growing to become one of the most populous in Europe. Meanwhile, Portarlington was becoming increasingly Anglican and, therefore, more of an Anglo-Irish town.

Left: Henri Massue(1648–1720), Marquis de Ruvigny and later Earl of Galway, who, before the Revocation, had been the Deputé Générale of the French Protestants at the French Court of Versailles. He was their chief lobbyist, the man they petitioned for favours and preferment, and he brought with him these skills, which were to be of enormous benefit to his co-religionists. He became undisputed leader of the Huguenot community in Britain and Ireland and was directly involved in the settlement of Portarlington in 1692.

Today, there are still Irish and Catholic families in the county who bear names such as Blanc and Champ, and families in other parts of Leinster, both Catholic and Protestant, whose Huguenot forebears gave them names such as Dubois, Perrin, Du Moulin and De Mange.

All that remains of the Portarlington French connection now are its meticulous records, a few of the old noble houses and an annual French Festival at which the wine of Bordeaux is imbibed in great quantities and snails and frogs legs are eaten in abundance, some by the English-speaking descendants of the original French settlers, but more by those of Gaelic and English origin.

Huguenots made a remarkable, if not fully recognized, contribution to Irish history. The less noble branches of the immigration, notably the weavers who established the Irish poplin industry, now vanished like the immigrants themselves, contributed greatly to the economy of a country which had been ravaged by more than half a century of warfare prior to their arrival. Their memory survives in a county of moorland and bog, pasture and parkland, in the heart of Ireland's Central Plain; a county of level land, except in the northwest where the Slieve Bloom mountains once housed rebel Gaelic chieftains.

Portarlington is now a backwater marked by cooling towers of a peat-powered electricity plant. The county town, Portlaois (formerly Maryborough) houses a giant prison, but the best place in which to lock yourself away with the memories of the French and their descendants is the town of Abbeyleix, planned in the 17th century by the local landlord, Viscount de Vesci, a nobleman of Norman descent. Here, on the main street, and not mentioned in the guidebooks, is Morrissey's pub, a halting place for the discerning imbiber, in a land where imbibers are discerning in the extreme. One of the most convivial and best-preserved bars in Ireland, it might just be the place to raise a glass of Bordeaux to the French who have passed on.

Below: The records in Portarlington's Eglise Française de St Paul (Church of St Paul) were kept in French from their first entry in 1694, until finally being superseded by English in 1816. Fortunately, these records were retained locally rather than sent to the Public Record Office in the Four Courts in Dublin whose priceless papers were destroyed in a fire during the civil war in the 1920s. As a result, more is known about the French who peopled Portarlington than is known of the Irish and Anglo-Irish who inhabited the rest of the county.

LONGFORD

Loveliest county of the plain

LONGFORD FIGURES LITTLE in the epic sagas of the *Ossianic* or *Ulster Cycles*, and it was never a strategic centre in the long history of battles, victories and defeats which other places have endured or exulted.

It is a quiet place, a place where water as often as land appears to make up the topography. Low hills, an abundance of lakes, streams and rivers flowing into the great River Shannon – which on its Longford shore takes on the appearance of a broad lake – and a man-made extra, in the form of the Royal Canal, give the county a watery aspect which is remarkable even in Ireland.

What remains of Oliver Goldsmith's body lies in the Poets' Corner in Westminster Abbey in London, where his epitaph, composed by Samuel Johnson reads: 'He touched nothing which he did not adorn.' His most prominent statue stands alongside that of Edmund Burke outside Trinity College, Dublin where he was educated. However, Goldsmith first saw the light of day in Pallas in the county of Longford, one of the least spectacular places in Ireland, but a region every bit as gentle and attractive as this quotation from his poem, 'Deserted Village ', suggests.

> *Sweet Auburn, loveliest village of the plain,*
> *Where health and plenty cheered the labouring swain,*
> *Where smiling spring its earliest visit paid,*
> *And parting summer's blooms delayed,*
> *Dear lovely bowers of innocence and ease,*
> *Seats of my youth, when every sport could please,*
> *How often have I loitered o'er thy green,*
> *Where humble happiness endeared each scene.*

FROM: 'DESERTED VILLAGE' BY OLIVER GOLDSMITH

Left: Fishing in the 'hot water stretch' of the River Shannon, and in Longford's many other loughs and rivers, provides the county's biggest tourist revenue.

The countryside abounds with places connected with the poet and author. At Pallas, his birthplace, there is a replica of Foley's Trinity College statue, and at Forgney Church, where his father, Revd Charles Goldsmith, was rector, there is a beautiful stained glass window depicting 'Sweet Auburn'.

As a young man, Goldsmith spent three years under the tutelage of Revd Patrick Hughes in Edgeworthstown, a place with another literary connection. The town was the seat of the Edgeworth family since 1583 and, in the 18th century, the scion was a Richard Lovell Edgeworth, an eccentric inventor and surveyor. One of his 24 children from his many marriages was Maria Edgeworth, the novelist, who wrote the much admired *Castle Rackrent*. Sir Walter Scott wrote in a preface to the Waverley Novels: 'I feel that something might be attempted for my own country of the same kind as that which Miss Edgeworth so fortunately achieved for Ireland'.

Another member of the extended family was the Abbé Edgeworth, a Roman Catholic priest, son of a Protestant clergyman, and a devotee of royalist France, who attended to the final religious needs of Louis XVI before he was executed, and later escaped to Russia.

Edgeworth House is now a nursing home, run by the religious Sisters of Mercy, who have maintained it in good condition, and the Edgeworth family vault is situated in the local St John's churchyard. Richard Lovell and Maria Edgeworth are buried there.

Longford figures strongly, too, in the Irish struggle for independence, and near Edgeworthstown one encounters a type of paradox which is not uncommon in Ireland.

Ballinalee was the home of General Sean McEoin, a guerrilla leader in the 1920s, known as the 'Blacksmith of Ballinalee', who was captured and sentenced to death on 14th June 1921. However, he was later released and eventually became Minister for Justice and Minister for Defence before unsuccessfully contesting two elections for the Presidency of Ireland.

Just south of Ballinalee is Currygrane, the birthplace of an Irishman of a very different political and religious hue. He was Field Marshal Sir

Right: Ardagh, the former mansion of Sir George Fetherston, which is reputed to have been instrumental in providing the plot for Oliver Goldsmith's comic play, She Stoops to Conquer, *the subtitle of which is 'The Mistakes of the Night'. The local story goes that one evening, Goldsmith, looking for an inn, asked to be directed to 'the best house in the village' whereupon he was sent to Squire Fetherston's. And that was only the first mistake of the night!*

Henry Wilson, Chief of the Imperial General Staff, who favoured repressive measures to crush militant Irish nationalism. Wilson was assassinated in London by Irish republicans in 1922.

Longford's newest attraction is in fact its oldest. In 1984, in a bog in the townland of Corlea, near the small town of Kenagh, 'trackway', made from large oak planks and dating from the early Iron Age, was discovered. Following excavation work four more 'trackways' were found. This was followed by the discovery of a further 16. Now 57 of these prehistoric roads have been uncovered in the area, and a major exhibition centre has been built at the site to inform visitors of the importance of these ancient remains.

The county town of Longford offers little in the way of architectural interest save for St Mel's Cathedral which has been described as one of the 'better post-emancipation churches' in Ireland. The architect, Augustus Welby Pugin, was less kind. It was, to his taste, 'A bad copy of that wretched compound of pagan and Protestant architecture, St Pancras New Church in London.'

Like most of Ireland's counties, Longford has been depopulated by emigration over the years, but the Longford emigration, like that of its neighbouring county of Westmeath, differs somewhat in that, as well as the traditional movements to Britain, North America and Australia, there was a considerable migration to Argentina from 1842 to 1860, during and after the Great Famine.

The Longford familes settled mainly in the province of Buenos Aires, where large tracts of land were being offered to European settlers. Edel Miro O'Farrell became President of the Republic of Argentina in 1914 and a kinsman of an even earlier emigrant, Romulo O'Farrill, is Mexico's leading media magnate.

LOUTH

A tale of brown bulls and battles

ASPUR OF MOUNTAINOUS GRANITE juts out like a thumb into the sea from the flat limestone plain of Louth, the smallest county in Ireland, to form the Cooley Peninsula. In ancient times, Louth was a borderland between the province of Ulster and, today, lies on the border of the Republic and Northern Ireland. Here, more than anywhere else in the province of Leinster, the landscape bears a resemblance to the jagged Atlantic coast. The pattern of settlement, too, is similar, and its barrier of mountains made it less open to the process of anglicization which quickly took hold elsewhere to the east of the River Shannon. The area around the picturesque village of Omeath was Gaelic-speaking into the beginning of this century, the last indigenous outpost of the ancient tongue in eastern Ireland.

The Cooley Peninsula, with its hills tumbling to the Irish Sea on the southern shore, and to Carlingford Lough on the north, is the site of one of the great epics of Irish mythology, the *Táin Bó Cuailgne*, 'the Cattle Raid of Cooley', which tells how Queen Maeve of Connacht set her forces, under the command of Ferdia, against those of his friend, Cuchullain of Louth, for the capture of a highly coveted bull owned by a Cooley farmer.

The exploits of all concerned were superhuman and the battles raged over vast stretches of territory; tops of mountains were sliced off by the swords of the combatants. Cuchullain, the epitome of epic heroes, slew hundreds of enemies single-handedly each day before the battle culminated in a four-day duel between him and his friend, Ferdia, at a place still known today as *Ardee Ath Fhirdia*, 'Ferdia's Ford'. Each night, regardless of the hostilities, Ferdia sent food and medicine across the ford to Cuchullain, until the third night when no messages were passed between the two men. On the fourth day Ferdia ran Cuchullain through

Left: Found at Monasterboice, this ornate Celtic cross and round tower are some of the remains of a monastry founded by St Buithe in the 5th century.

127

with his sword and gravely wounded him, but Cuchullain finally produced the *coup-de-grâce* with his magic spear, the *Gae Bulgach*, and Ferdia was no more.

As all this went on, the wily Queen Maeve had smuggled the Brown Bull of Cooley back across the Shannon to Connacht, so the two friends had fought, and Ferdia had died, in vain. True to a tradition in which words were as potent as weapons, the conflict ended with Cuchullain reciting an encomium over the body of his friend in which he praised his opponent's courage and lamented the death of a great hero.

Over in Connacht, Maeve had a surprise waiting for her, the Brown Bull of Cooley having entered into his own personal battle with the white-horned bull belonging to her husband, Ailell, which he killed before heading back eastwards to his beloved hills of Cooley. For all its heroism the *Táin* also carries a subtext on the futility of war.

The southern part of Louth has its seaside resorts and its historic connotations, centred mainly on the town of Drogheda where the River Boyne completes its journey to the sea. Down river on the north bank from the town is Baltray, home of one of the finest golf links in Ireland. The East of Ireland Amateur Championship, one of the four major provincial golf competitions in the country, takes place here annually.

Drogheda itself is remembered historically for the lack of quarter given to its residents by its most unpopular tourist, Oliver Cromwell, in 1649. At that time Sir Arthur Aston held Drogheda for King Charles I against the Roundheads, and on 10th September the town fell to Cromwell's third assault. Cromwell, a symbol of democracy in most parts of the world, was a man of his time, an era when the line between progress and barbarity was thinly drawn. He ordered the execution of some 2000 of the town's defenders, including Aston, and many of the survivors were transported to the West Indies.

In the 12th century, Drogheda's strategic position near the mouth of the Boyne was not wasted on the Anglo-Norman colonists who set up a castle and a bridge here, and by the Middle Ages, Drogheda, along with Dublin, was one of the most important English towns in Ireland. There was even a parliament which passed an Act, in 1465, for the setting up of a Drogheda University.

Although Drogheda's significance would diminish over the centuries,

Right: St Brigid, Dundalk, Louth. The patroness of Ireland, St Brigid, who was born at Faughart, four miles (6.5 km) north of Dundalk, founded the great abbey of Kildare and comes after St Patrick and before St Columba in the hierarchy of patron saints of the Irish. She is remembered throughout Ireland in the form of an irregular cross made from rushes, known as St Brigid's cross, which hangs on the walls of many an Irish living room.

Left: Oliver Cromwell (1599–1658).
His arrival in Ireland in 1649,
following the execution of Charles I,
heralded his final brutal campaign of
the civil war during which he ruthlessly
avenged the murder of Protestants by
Catholic rebels in 1641 with the
sacking of Drogheda and Wexford
(drawing by Henry Ford).

there are still some magnificent architectural examples extant of the town's former splendour. The most impressive of these is St Lawrence's Gate, a magnificent barbican complex at the junction of St Lawrence Street and Palace Street, with its pair of great circular towers linked by double arches and topped by a battlement.

In more recent times, parts of Louth have formed the borderlands with Northern Ireland in the course of the 'Troubles'. Moments of carnage, such as the deaths, in 1979, of eight British paratroopers near the narrow stretch of water in Warrenpoint – a place clearly seen from Cooley – and, in true Irish fashion, moments of comedy too, as when a detachment of Britain's most feared professional troops, the Special Air Service (SAS), was arrested by a village policeman in Omeath after they strayed across the border claiming they did not know how to read their maps.

For the moment all is peaceful in this borderland. The most sought after shells in the beautiful fishing port of Carlingford, where the 1935 foot (590 m) Slieve Foye Mountain tumbles into the sea, are those of the local oysters and prawns which are washed down with Guinness or Harp lager from a brewery in the county town of Dundalk.

MEATH

A seat of kings

THE FENIAN CYCLE, Ireland's equivalent of the mythology of the Greeks and the sagas of the Norsemen, tells tales of great heroism, of *Tír na n'Og*, 'the land of the young', an island to the west whose inhabitants never grow old, and of the great tragic love story of Diarmuid and Grainne.

The place at the centre of these great tales was Tara, a name indelible in the minds and hearts of the Irish. It was not in any way accidental that the great house in which the heroine of *Gone with the Wind*, Scarlet O'Hara, was raised was given this name by her Irish father. No name could have been more synonymous with his Irishness.

All that remains of Tara today is a green meadow on a low hilltop, rutted with earthworks which provide the few discernible traces of the presence of a distant glory. All that is now gone, as the romantic poet Thomas Moore wrote:

> *No more to chiefs and ladies bright,*
> *The harp of Tara swells,*
> *The cord alone that breaks at night*
> *Its tale of ruin tells,*
> *Thus Freedom now so seldom wakes,*
> *The only throb she gives,*
> *Is when some heart indignant breaks,*
> *To show that she still lives.*

FROM: 'THE HARP THAT ONCE THROUGH TARA'S HALLS' BY THOMAS MOORE

The visitor to Tara now must come equipped with imagination; the ability to picture the great banqueting hall of King Cormac Mac Airt, close to

Left: A centre for pagan worship from about 2100 BC, Tara became 'a seat of kings' in the 6th century when it was taken over by the ruling Uí Néill dynasty.

Right: Dublin-born Thomas Moore (1779–1852) was a poet and satirist. His most famous work was Irish Melodies, *a collection of 130 poems which included such familiar titles as 'The Last Rose of Summer' and 'The Harp that once through Tara's Halls the Soul of Music Spread'. These were set to the music of Moore and Sir John Stevenson and performed for London's aristocracy where they aroused much sympathy for the Irish nationalists, among whom Thomas Moore was a popular hero.*

half a mile (0.9 km) in length, where the kings became gods through a symbolic ritual mating with the Earth Goddess while their warriors feasted.

The hall, the *Teach Midhchuarta*, was believed to have been divided into five aisles, according to the medieval chroniclers. In the central aisle stood the great cauldrons, the fires for roasting and the flaming torches. On either side were aisles with booths in which the host's guests sat, in places allocated according to the nobility of their birth and their current social status.

Other pagan ceremonies included the games and fair, *Aonach Tailte*, which were held on the Hill of Tailte about half-way between the market towns of Navan and Kells. The foot races and the throwing of weights continued at this site for centuries into the Christian era and were held formally for the last time under the patronage of Roderick O'Connor, the High King of Ireland, in 1168, one year before the arrival of the Norman knights from Britain. In the early years of Irish independence, romantics in the new Irish Free State attempted to revive the games, but their efforts at mock-Celticism quickly petered out.

Another great festival of the ancient Celts was *Samhain,* which was held every three years on the Hill of Ward, overlooking the County Meath town of Athboy, on the eve of a pagan feast, the night known to us now as Hallowe'en. This was a wild and savage occasion with human sacrifices offered and victims burned as offerings by the druids to the gods; this was the true 'Hallowe'en 1', far more frightening than the most horrific of horror movies.

These old Celtic traditions and the places intimately associated with them are, for all their mysticism, for all their embellishment over the millennia, younger than other more mysterious traditional places in this county. Along the banks of the Boyne, and particularly in the area surrounding one large loop of its journey to the Irish Sea, an unknown people settled; their great burial grounds, some nearly 5000 years old, remain.

Who these people were, no one knows, but they knew of the cycles of the sun and they buried their chieftains in splendour. The complex at Newgrange has been dated scientifically to be from 3100 BC. Each year, on the days around 21st December – the winter solstice – a shaft of light penetrates the dark, 30 yard (27 m) passageway and focuses on the very centre of the tomb chamber. The precision of the event and the design of the 'roof box' through which the sun's rays are admitted, rule out suggestions of a fluke, an accident, a mere coincidence. The great chamber, it seems, was designed 5000 years ago as a solar observatory.

The arrival of the sun's light at the very doors of the dead on the shortest days of the year must have symbolized rebirth and renewal; new light and new hope to the not-so-primitive people who lived in the bend of the Boyne.

From where did those people come? Legend is virtually unanimous that the earliest inhabitants of Ireland arrived directly from Spain, the land of the sun. More likely, however, is the far less romantic but more scientific notion that they made their way from continental Europe by the shortest sea routes: across the English Channel and the narrow sea between the southernmost tips of Scotland and the northeast coast of Ireland. Wherever they came from, they found their way to Meath; to the centre of the mystical in Ireland; to the valley of the River Boyne which saw the birth of Celtic myth, legend and civilization in Ireland, but also witnessed its death.

At the town of Oldbridge, not far from Newgrange, on the first day of July in the year of 1690, two great armies faced one another across the river. On the northern bank stood 36,000 Dutch, English, Danish and German troops loyal to King William III and the reformed Protestant religion; to the south the ground was held by 26,000 mainly Irish and French soldiers loyal to William's father-in-law, the Stuart king, James II, and the Catholic faith.

Below: The sun hitting the famous threshold stone just below the entrance to the 66 feet (20 m) long passage grave which leads to the ancient tomb chamber at Newgrange. The chamber itself measures 280 feet (85 m) in diameter and has an extraordinary 20 feet (6 m) high corbeled vaulted roof. The symbolism of the decorations on the outer stones at Newgrange and those lining the chamber continues to puzzle the experts, although it is thought that the spirals could be a symbol of the labyrinthine path to the underworld and that the concentric circles might be connected with sun worship.

Above: The fair held by Trim Castle, Ireland's largest Anglo-Norman fortress.

Left: Donapatrick Church on the banks of the River Blackwater. St Patrick brought Christianity to Ireland in the 5th century.

Among the first to run when the battle swung in William's favour was James himself, although, his army remained intact to fight again at Aughrim in County Galway a year later – and this time to lose more disastrously. The old Gaelic civilization, debilitated 89 years earlier by defeat at Kinsale, in County Cork (where, incidentally, James had landed to begin his campaign) was now on its last legs. The landed Catholic familes fled to the continent just as the losers at Kinsale, the Ulster princes of the O'Neill and O'Donnell lines, had done following that earlier defeat.

O'Neill and O'Donnell, the earls of Tyrone and Tyrconnell, left for Spain; those defeated at the Boyne went initially to France and spread from there throughout Europe. Some of them, and their descendants, did well for themselves. Richard Hennessy and his successors prospered in the region of Cognac; the Taaffe family provided a first minister to the Habsburgs.

Those left behind were less fortunate. Lands and estates were lost; the peasantry – not that their lot was prosperous under their indigenous landlords – fell into despair and a destitution unparallelled in western Europe. Old traditions petered out. The stories of former glory lived on but were told in the English language and thus diminished from great saga to tales spoken in impoverished cabins.

Ironically, Meath today is the only county in the province of Leinster where the Gaelic tongue is still spoken as the vernacular. The Gaeltacht region in the parish of Rath Chairn near Athboy is not, however, the result of the tenacity of a small group of the indigenous population, but stems from a social experiment of the 1930s in which families from the beautiful region of Connemara left their infertile, rocky and tiny parcels of land in the west to take up small-holdings on an estate which was divided amongst them.

Unlike the rest of Gaelic-speaking Ireland, where the ancient language is in peril, the number of Irish speakers in Rath Chairn is growing as time goes on. Thus the language still lives, albeit artificially, in the cradle of Gaelic civilization.

THE PROVINCE OF LEINSTER

Right: Fairyhouse in County Meath, home of the Irish Grand National, is one of Ireland's premier racecourses. First run in 1870, when it was won by Sir Robert Peel owned by Mr L. Dunne, the Grand National quickly became Ireland's most valuable and prestigious steeplechase. Over the years each race has had its own rich tale, none more amazing than the win in 1929 of a six-year-old mare, Alike, owned and ridden by Frank Wise who was missing three fingers and who rode with a wooden leg.

OFFALY

Reaching for the stars

THE COUNTY OF OFFALY is best known for its stretches of bogland and for its wild Slieve Blooms, which, rare for Irish mountains, are not close to the sea. It is also the site of 'St Kieran's City' at Clonmacnois, on the banks of the Shannon, where the impressive remains of a large and significant monastic settlement, dating from 545 AD, describe a time when it was a centre of Celtic learning, literature and art, an era when most of the rest of Europe was being engulfed by the barbarian invasions.

Another of Offaly's sources of repute rests in the demesne of Birr Castle, home of the Parsons family, earls of Rosse for 14 generations. Here in its Gothic-style housing lies the tube of what was, from the 1840s until 1917, the greatest telescope in the world, the 'Leviathan of Birr' which was constructed by Lord Oxmantown (later the 3rd Earl of Rosse) in 1845.

In the first half of the 19th century when work began there had been a tradition of secrecy among the experts in glass and mirror-making, so Oxmantown, deciding to make his mirror from metal rather than glass, built a forge and enlisted the services of a blacksmith, a carpenter and labourers from his own estate. He then invented a steam-driven apparatus to polish the metal, and the final result, known as the 'Three Foot Telescope', was installed in 1839.

However, within a year, plans were already underway to build an even greater telescope. In 1840, Dr Thomas Romney Robinson, director of the Armagh Observatory, reported that, 'Lord Oxmantown is about to construct a telescope of unequalled dimensions. He intends it to be six feet aperture and fifty feet focus . . . his character is an assurance that it will be devoted, in the most unreserved manner, to the service of astronomy, while the energy that could accomplish such a triumph and the liberality that has placed his discoveries in this difficult art within

Left: Bog cotton, found in Offaly's peat bogs which cover 34 per cent of the county and provide raw materials for generating electricity.

139

reach of all, may justly be reckoned among the highest distinctions of Ireland.'

Work on the mirror presented, according to Robinson, a spectacle of 'sublime beauty' in which 'furnaces poured out huge columns of nearly monochromatic yellow flame, and the ignited crucibles during their passage through the air were fountains of red light, producing on the towers of the castle and the foliage of the trees, such accidents of colour and shade as might almost transport fancy to the planets of a constrasted double star.'

On 13th April 1842 the vast mirror had been cast. By February 1845 the great tube was in place and had been officially opened by Dean Peacock of the Church of Ireland who, to demonstrate its great size, paraded through it wearing his top hat and carrying his umbrella above his head.

The occasion was a great one, but its timing was inauspicious. In that year the potato crop was blighted and Ireland's Great Famine was underway. The earl, who sat as a representative Irish peer in the House of Lords in Westminster, ceased his astronomic activites and devoted his time to relief work. The 'Leviathan' was left virtually unused until 1848 when the worst of the famine was over and the population of the country had collapsed through hunger, disease and emigration.

From the 1850s onwards, the fame of the telescope began to spread. The opening of the railways made Birr more accessible and the visitors' book at Birr Castle, intact today, recorded those who came to gaze further into space than was possible anywhere else on earth. A special feature in *The Illustrated London News* extended the fame of the 'Leviathan'.

The first entry is devoted to the visit of Charles Babbage, the scientist and inventor of the mechanical calculator, who came to see the stars on

Below: An illustration of 'The Great Rosse Telescope' as it appeared in The Illustrated London News *on 19th April 1845.*

Left: East of Birr, the heathery ridges
of the Slieve Bloom mountains mark
the border between County Offaly and
County Laois. Standing out as they do,
the only interruption of a low horizon,
they appear quite imposing, although
in fact the highest point in the range is
only about 1700 feet (520 m).

9th September 1850 and was followed quickly by a Mr John Morrison of New York, Professor E.J. Santamour of Geneva and, with a flourish, Le Chevalier Sigismund Neukomm of Geneva who arrived at this place set among the peat bogs of central Ireland in August 1852. Many others followed from places as far afield as St Petersburg and Budapest. The voyages made by Dr Browne from Van Diemens Land (now Tasmania) in 1854 and that by the first New Zealander recorded in the visitors' book, a certain Mr Studholme, in 1892, beggar description.

When these intrepid astromers arrived at Birr their problems were by no means over. There was often cloud and consequently long waits for the night skies to clear. Mirrors became tarnished and had to be removed for polishing. All in all, it was a business that required not only painstaking study and endurance, but also a great deal of patience.

So it continued into the early years of the 20th century until, in 1916, Birr's full time astronomer, Otto Boeddicker, from Germany, was forced to leave Ireland as an 'enemy alien' in the course of the First World War. A year later a larger telescope than the Leviathan was built at Mount Wilson in the United States with a 100 inch (254 cm) reflector and the great days of Birr had ended.

But in the three-quarters of a century of its operation the great telescope made remarkable contributions to the science of astronomy. The 3rd Earl of Rosse had died in 1866 having left behind fine drawings of the planets and having discovered the spiral nature of nebulae.

The small market town took its important visitors in its stride. It had been laid out by the earlier members of the Parsons family in the 18th century with a neat square and the fine Georgian Oxmantown Mall which leads to the entrance of the castle and its demesne.

A statue of the Duke of Cumberland, scourge of the Jacobites, had been commissioned to be placed on a Doric column in the centre of the square but was never erected. The column stands bare to this day. The buildings of the town's centre exude the classical elegance of their period and perhaps the finest is 'John's Hall', an Ionic temple, built in 1828 to the memory of John Clere Parsons, the 3rd Earl's brother, a brilliant mathmatician, who died of typhoid in his twenties.

Close by, on John's Mall, stands the fine statue, by John Henry Foley, of William Parsons, the 3rd Earl of Rosse, who made his front lawn the centre of world astronomy, and who shared his discoveries and his great telescope with all who expressed a serious interest in the science.

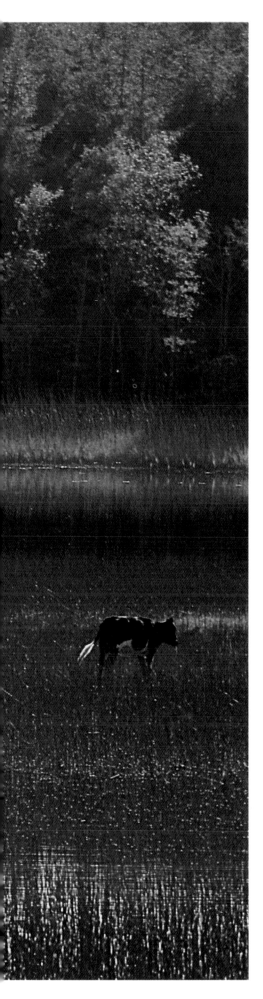

WESTMEATH

With its 'golden voice'

WESTMEATH WAS HIVED OFF from the ancient province of Meath to become a separate county by a decree of Henry VIII which declared: 'For as much as the shire of Meath is great and large and the west part thereof is beset with divers of the King's enemies and his writs have not been obeyed, in consideration thereof it is thought meet that the said shire should be divided.'

In short, the Gaelic way of life had persisted longer here than in most of the province of Leinster. The chieftains with their poets, bards and musicians lingered on in this region, which borders on the still-Gaelic province of Connacht.

Two market towns today dominate this intensely rural county which is famous mainly for its beef herds, but also for one man who took the musical world by storm in the early part of this century.

It is certain that somewhere, silently, in an attic near you, there is a 'golden voice', first heard in County Westmeath in 1884. Our grandfathers and, more particularly, our grandmothers – for the voice belonged to a 'fine figure of a man' – whether in Ireland, Britain, the United States or further afield in Australia and New Zealand, might have collected the records of the tenor, John McCormack. Some of them may still be in your own attic to this day.

It is a long artistic way from the narrow streets of Athlone, Ireland's most central town, to the auditoriums of the *Teatro alla Scala* in Milan and the Metropolitan and Carnegie Hall in New York, but that is the journey McCormack made.

His parents, Scottish-born of Irish origin, had returned to the 'old country' where his father obtained work at the Athlone woollen mills. Their son was a bright lad who gained a scholarship to a boarding school in Sligo, won several singing competitions but was astute enough to

Left: Cattle graze by the River Inny in Westmeath which, like Offaly, Laois, Longford and Roscommon, consists largely of bog, pasture and lots of water.

realize that his tenor voice needed training, and that Italy was the place where the job should be done.

He set about raising the funds to achieve this and, after some months tuition with Maestro Vincenzo Sabbatini, made his debut as a 22-year-old in the title role of Mascagni's *L'Amico Fritz* in the *Teatro Chiabrero* in Savona.

After that bright start things went badly, but McCormack was a tough working-class boy from Athlone at a time when Ireland was one of the poorest countries in Europe and Athlone was by no means to be counted among its more prosperous centres. He was full of determination to make a name for himself and, according to those who knew him, was possessed of 'language so earthy a docker might blush to hear him.' Odd, is it not, that the tongue which held a voice which rivalled that of Caruso, which lilted the muscial phrases of Mozart's *Il Mio Tesoro*, could be capable of strong language that could put a stevedore to shame?

It is odd too that the rivalry between McCormack and Caruso was of the friendliest of natures. No hard feelings were entertained. Each tenor deferred to the other as the greatest of the day. Both became millionaires, of course, and both became mainstays of the RCA Victor recording company. The rivals were also personal friends.

But there was more to it than that. Caruso was an actor and an artist, as shown by his affectionate caricatures of McCormack in pen and ink. Caruso excelled in the flamboyant settings of Grand Opera. McCormack was a bad actor, but was the master of the individual concert appearance.

McCormack's success was phenonemal. He was the first mega-star of music and this success led to a mansion in Hollywood and a grand estate

Right: John McCormack (1884–1945), one of the finest and most popular tenor singers of the first quarter of the 20th century, was born in Athlone, in County Westmeath, to Andrew and Hannah McCormack, the fourth of eleven children. In 1906 he married Lily Foley, a Dublin soprano, with whom he had two children, a son, Cyril, and a daughter, Gwen. In 1920, having spent several years in the USA, he returned to Dublin with his family where he lived until his death on 16th September 1945. Today the 'John McCormack Golden Voice Competition', which is held every year in Athlone, in his memory, attracts top-grade singers from Britain and Ireland.

in Ireland which was once the seat of the earls of Drogheda. He, too, was ennobled by being made a Count of the Papal Court, and for a great part of his life was known as 'John, Count McCormack', or simply as 'the Count', to his thousands of admirers.

He was lionized in America, being the guest of honour at President Wilson's Fourth of July concert in 1918, having a year previously renounced 'all previous allegiances' to the United Kingdom – which included Ireland – to become an American citizen. This act was virtually ignored in Ireland, but, officially, England took offence, as his change of nationality had taken place a few months before America had entered the 'Great War'. There was an irony here, too, for it was in England, after his voice and his fortune had failed, that his most loyal audiences remained.

Failure of voice was a natural phenomenon, but the failure of fortune was self-inflicted, with the help of a weakness for slow racehorses. The story persists of a meeting on The Curragh in County Kildare between the trainer of 'the Count's' expensive charges and a stable boy.

'I thought you would be in Dublin today, sir,' the boy suggested. 'Why, son?' asked the trainer. 'The Count is singing in the Theatre Royal, sir,' the boy replied. This elicted the immortal response: 'My dear boy, when we are finished with him, your Count shall be singing *outside* the Theatre Royal.'

It didn't quite end up like that, but the young man who set out from Westmeath to conquer the world was, to a large extent, successful in his quest before the world conquered him. Having achieved world-wide fame in the sphere in which he was talented, he, in his insecurity, sought fame in a sphere, that of the turf, in which his talents were limited in the extreme. Still, his memory remains in the minds of the operatic *cognoscenti* and his voice, in brittle Bakelite, lies in the attics of Westmeath and the world.

Above: A horse fair in County Westmeath. Horses have always been an important part of life in Ireland. As far back as the pre-Christian era legend has it that the Red Branch Knights rode on horseback. The two best-known Irish breeds are the Connemara pony and the Irish Draught, a heavy working horse, which has been crossed with the thoroughbred to produce some superb Irish hunters.

145

WEXFORD

Crucible of the 1798 rebellion

WEXFORD IS TRULY a place apart. It is separated by natural barriers from the rest of Ireland but with close connections by sea to Britain and to mainland Europe. For this reason the county has provided access to immigrants from abroad from the earliest times; to invading armies later. Now, at Rosslare, it provides ferry connections to South Wales and to Le Havre and Cherbourg in France.

It was in Wexford, in 1169, that the Anglo-Norman conquest of Ireland began. This was followed by settlers from England and Wales. Here, as well as the Gaelic surnames of Kinsella, Murphy, O'Connor and Kehoe, can be found families called Dake, Fleming, Devereux, Furlong, and Harvey.

For centuries Wexford has been mainly an English-speaking county. Even in the 1798 rebellion, when the county rose up against British rule, the rebels tended to be English speakers, while their loyalist opponents included Gaelic-speaking militia from the province of Munster.

Today, the English language is delivered in Wexford with a unique accent. In earlier time, in certain parts of the county, people conversed in a dialect known as 'Yola', which bore strong resemblance to that of Somerset in England, especially regarding the tendency to pronounce the letter 'S' as 'Z'. Remnants of the old way of speaking persist in the southern baronies of Forth and Bargy, a flat sea-bound area entwined with little roads.

The English of Ireland is full of dialect words, but in the vast majority of cases these are survivors from the Gaelic which was once the dominant language. What makes Wexford, and Forth and Bargy in particular, different in its speech from most of the rest of the country, is that the dialect words are essentially English in origin, with some Flemish undertones to complicate matters further.

Left: Wexford town stands on a site occupied from the 9th to the 12th centuries by the Vikings who founded the flourishing port of Waesfjord.

Above: Prisoners being executed on Wexford Bridge on 21st June 1798. The causes of the Wexford insurrection had their roots in such hardships as land hunger, increased taxes and a crisis in the local agrarian economy (notably the grain market). The surprising emergence of several members of the gentry as local leaders in the rising indicates that it was not just the poor who felt alienated by years of repressive government.

To *keek* is to peep, to prime a water pump is to *hench* it, if there is a cold easterly wind it is a '*hash* day'. Wexford is famous, too, for its 'mummers' – bands of singers who move from house to house at certain times of year. It is also home to the country's only indigenous Christmas Carol, 'The Wexford Carol'. All those traditions have been imported from abroad, as have the blood-lines of many of the people, yet Wexford is essentially Irish, as Irish as anywhere in Ireland and more Irish than most places.

In the summer of 1798, inspired by the ideals of the United Irishmen (a nationalist group imbued with the spirit of the French and American revolutions), the Catholic peasantry of Wexford united against loyalist forces in a war of short duration but intense bloodiness. The rebels had some spectacular successes early on and fought bravely in the hope of a landing by sympathetic French forces. However, it was all over in six weeks. The Wexford rebels, armed with pikes, were defeated by the might of loyalist forces in the form of regular soldiers, mercenaries from Hesse and a tough regiment of the north Cork militia, and treated brutally in that defeat. Towards the end, the idealism of the rebels had degenerated into sectarianism, the major outrage being the burning alive of Protestant loyalist families in a barn in the townland of Scullabogue. The French landed at Killala in County Mayo six weeks after the rising in Wexford had been put down. Their intervention was too small and too far away to make any difference.

Bitterness and repression haunted the county for many years after that fateful summer and, even today, the year of 1798 is still engraved on the hearts of the people of Wexford. It was the greatest calamity in the history of a county which was spared the worst of the Great Famine in the 19th century. Almost every Wexford town and village has its commemorative statue of a 1798 rebel, pike in hand.

What's the news, what's the news
Oh my bold Shelmalier,
With your long-barrelled gun of the sea.
Goodly news, goodly news,
Do I bring youth of Forth,
Goodly news do I bring Bargy man,
For the boys march at dawn,
From the South to the North,
Led by Kelly the boy from Killane.

BALLAD OF THE WEXFORD REBELS OF 1798

The county town of Wexford is one of delightful, narrow streets in which some famous people and some interesting people were born. Jane Francis Elgee, mother of Oscar Wilde, was born in Wexford town and her epigrams were almost as famous as her son's. On 'respectability', for example, she is reputed to have said: 'Respectability is for tradesmen. We [the Wildes] are above respectability.'

But the true character of Wexford is shaped by the sea. There is a seafaring tradition here which is stronger than anywhere else in Ireland, with the possible exception of the town of Arklow in the neighbouring county of Wicklow, and this latter is truly an extension of the Wexford tradition.

The Irish Sea coast along the east of the county and the small Atlantic coastline to the south, which are dotted with beaches and quaint villages with their local pubs, has become the prime holiday haunt of Dubliners. It is close enough for a day trip, yet far enough to be completely uncontaminated by the city.

Almost the entire coast of Wexford is important in the ornithological sphere. The North Slob, hardly an enticing name, is situated across the bridge from Wexford town and contains the Wexford Wildfowl Reserve, where 30 per cent of the world's Greenland white-fronted geese spend their winters. Perhaps this is no wonder since Wexford has more hours of sunshine annually than anywhere else in Ireland.

Left: Commodore John Barry (1745–1803), who won significant victories during the American War of Independence, was born in Ballysampson in County Wexford. He later became known as the 'Father of the United States Navy' for training so many young officers who later became celebrated in America's history. This commanding statue of him stands on Wexford town quay.

149

Right: Ethereal in the dawn light, the North Slob comprises 2400 acres (971 ha) of reclaimed land which came into being in 1849 when a local benefactor, John Edward Redmond, built a hefty embankment north of Wexford harbour and drained the land behind it. An even larger area south of the harbour, South Slob, was drained in 1856. The overall result of this ambitious venture was 5000 acres of prime agricultural land, 8 feet (2.4 m) below sea level, albeit at the cost of access to the harbour by anything but the smallest or flat-bottomed boats. A consequence of the dyke was that an estimated annual 570 million tonnes of shallow tidal waters, which previously flowed in and out of the harbour mouth helping to maintain the depth of the channels, were no longer available.

WICKLOW

The 'Garden of Ireland'

A**T POWERSCOURT** in Enniskerry in County Wicklow, a mere 12 miles (19 km) from the bustling centre of Dublin, the pointed Sugarloaf Mountain provides a perfect backdrop for the man-made lake with its fountain, its terraces and its statues of Pegasus, with the effect that the gardens appear to lead naturally and seamlessly to the true countryside. No line of division can be perceived.

Nowhere else in Ireland could this have been possible; certainly not in the ruggedness of the Atlantic coast where the contrast between the gentility of the 18th-century Anglo-Irish landscapers and the savage grandeur of the terrain would have been impossible to reconcile.

But Wicklow is the 'Garden of Ireland'. Its scenery is naturally graduated; the great massif slopes gently to the sea on the east and to the Central Plain on the west. Here, there are no great cliffs battered by the ocean's rage, no deep inlets, no craggy shores, but instead sloping pastures filled with black-faced sheep ushered from pasture to pasture by the slender-faced Wicklow collie. Where Wicklow reaches the sea there are long beaches, some of them, such as the three-mile (5 km) strand at Brittas Bay, crowded at weekends because of their proximity to Dublin, but others, known to a few, virtually empty whatever the weather and whatever the day of the week.

Wicklow, the county town, is also a Viking foundation and takes its name from that of the 9th century settlement, *Vikingalo*. Now, long after the northern warriors have departed into history, Wicklow is a small port and a seaside town set in gentle countryside.

Rugged beauty does exist, but mainly in the deserted centre, on the crests of Ireland's largest mountain chain, where Dubliners, at weekends in summer, hew peat, and picnic, and fill their lungs and, on the occasional clear day, view the mountain tops of Snowdonia in Wales.

Left: Another town that was founded by the Vikings, Arklow has lost its former importance as a port and is better known today for its yacht-building.

Above: Charles Stewart Parnell (1846–91) (cartoon by Amand) who was elected to Parliament in 1875 as an advocate of Home Rule for Ireland. Grim and autocratic, his status as a Protestant landlord gave credibility to his rhetorical assault on his own class, and in 1877, having been made president of the Home Rule Confederation of Great Britain, he became the most conspicuous figure in Irish politics. His subsequent political manoeuvres helped bring Gladstone to the office of Prime Minister and, in 1886, a proposal for Home Rule before the House of Commons. In 1890–91, following a public scandal involving him with Kitty O'Shea, the wife of one of his colleagues, he lost much of his standing in Ireland. He died suddenly in October 1891.

Right: The ruined church at Baltinglass which, together with the cloister, is all that remains of the important 12th-century Cistercian monastery, Vallis Salutis, 'Vale of Health'. Adorned with remarkable capitals, carved in typically Irish designs, this institution inspired the creation of many other monasteries in the area.

The rest of the county slopes gently to the sea, its great houses and gardens nestling in valleys and glens which were gouged from the land in the harsh Ice Age, but which now provide generous micro-climates in which palms and yuccas are able to flourish, albeit at the northernmost limits of their existence.

From the time of the Norman conquest 800 years ago – a mere millisecond in the Irish historical mind – the families which ousted the O'Byrnes and O'Tooles from their traditional lands, settled, discarded their rough colonial ways and, in succeeding generations, opened their hearts and minds to the land and culture which surrounded them.

Before all that there had been houses and gardens in Wicklow, notably in the great 6th century monastic settlement established by St Coemgen, 'Kevin', in Glendalough, 'the valley of two lakes'. After Kevin's death in 619 AD the monastery continued to flourish through the centuries. It began to decline following an attack by the English of Dublin in 1389, but was not finally put down until the conquest of Wicklow by the English in the 15th and 16th centuries.

The unused buildings, and there are so many of them that the place has been described as a 'monastic city', then fell into decay. The more enlightened hands of the restorers of the Office of Public Works have been in action since 1873 and have saved the settlement with its chapels, cathedral and hermitages from total ruin.

Kevin was, of course, a holy man and celibate, according to legend, to the point of violence. The stories say that he once flung an aspiring temptress to her death from the heights above the lakes.

Much later, another man of Wicklow, in times of greater sophistication, was to take a woman to his heart instead of dashing her to the rocks with consequences which led to one of the great personal and political tragedies of the 19th century.

Charles Stewart Parnell was born at Avondale, near Rathdrum, in 1846, the year that saw Ireland broken by the Great Famine. In 1875, he took his place in the House of Commons, in Westminster, where he devoted his life to returning the seat of power in Ireland to College Green whence it had been wrested in a welter of bribery in the final days of the 18th century.

Many of the 'honourable' members had accepted hard cash to relieve their encumbered estates, while others were tempted by 'ennoblement' and accepted 'Union Peerages' in return for their votes which dissolved the Irish parliament and created the United Kingdom of Great Britain and Ireland.

Intent on undoing their work, Parnell succeeded in casting a spell on his country. He was 'our poor dead king' to Joyce; the 'uncrowned king of Ireland' to the dispossessed peasantry; and finally the tormented leader, politically broken by his love for Kitty O'Shea, the wife of a fellow member of the nationalist Irish Party at Westminster.

The 'Parnell Affair' carved the heart of the nationalist cause in two, with provincial Ireland, a geographical pocket or two apart, and its Roman Catholic clergy, denouncing him as an adulterer, and Dublin's open-hearted artisans, strongly supporting the 'poor king' until his untimely death.

Avondale is an elegant 'Big House' of its time, set in 500 acres (202 ha) of tranquil and pleasant woods and gardens. Its true significance, however, and overwhelming attraction, stems from the great man who was born and lived there; the poignant redolence of a great political and personal tragedy is its strongest feature. A place of beauty mixed with sadness and tragedy, it captures the soul of Ireland.

Left: Bray Head, whose name derives from the Gaelic, Bri Cualann, meaning 'the hill of Cuala', rises out of the sea to a height of 791 feet (241 m) above the town of Bray in County Wicklow. Situated only a few miles south of Dublin, with a golden strand which stretches for over a mile (1.6 km), Bray is one of Ireland's biggest and longest established seaside resorts.

THE PROVINCE OF
CONNACHT

FOR ABOUT 25 YEARS after the War of Independence between Britain and Ireland, which resulted in the Anglo-Irish Treaty, approved in *Dail Eireann* on 7th January 1922, what is now the Republic of Ireland was officially called the Irish Free State – a fine name indeed.

While the title has long since been replaced, I would argue gently that, in its most literal sense, the Irish Free State still exists, in a very real way, inside those allegedly merely geographic boundaries of the province of Connacht. Certainly, visitors from Northern Ireland, when summer comes, pour into Connacht in their tens of thousands and always refer to it, in their sharpened accents, as the 'free state'.

Connacht is in many ways indeed the 'Irish free state'. It is 'Ballyescape'. It is for holidays; for feasting the eyes, and the spirit. It is for what we call 'the Craic'. It is the place where the clocks seem to run without the urgencies of elsewhere. It is the region where some mysterious alchemy has subtly married the best of Ireland's yesterworlds to the better elements of a nation's social and economic progress. Although by far the poorest of the provinces economically, it is, by common consent, infinitely the richest in what it has to offer those who come to see, to hear, to smell, to touch; to taste the core of a culture.

Gaelic is still the musical mother tongue in parts of Connemara, as it is on many of the offshore islands where the tough, yet delicate, *currachs* nimbly dance their darkened shadows from wavetip to spumed trough, durable as the culture itself. There are more musicians per acre, of flute and fiddle and accordion, than anywhere else, except maybe in County Clare. In the quietest corners of the great mountains of the west there are still hardy bands of moonshiners servicing a ritual which, though illegal, is almost as old as the hills themselves. Hay is still cut and saved the old slow way on many of the small farms; more turf is burned aromatically

Left: Bathed in midsummer sun, a Connemara funeral group follows the coffin to a seaside cemetery at Carraroe in County Galway.

159

through old and venerable chimneys; salmon are still poached from the rivers as they have always been poached, and the huntsmen and women of The Galway Blazers still ride as recklessly pell-mell as they ever did. Yet, there is a modern factory just around the corner, its spaces full of new cars; a new hotel tucked cunningly, almost unseen, against the side of that mountain; supertrawlers costing £10 million sharing the seas with the *currachs* and bright new bungalows facing setting suns with golden windows.

This rugged unofficial 'Irish free state' now attracts more tourists annually than even fabled Killarney. A few are so captivated that they never leave again. The coastline areas of Galway and Mayo, from which, ironically, many natives still emigrate, are now liberally dotted with colonies of mainly European young people. They, like the Norman invaders of centuries past, are well on their way to becoming more Irish than the Irish themselves.

Galway and Mayo, Sligo and Roscommon and lovely little languid Leitrim, these are the stops along the twisting road which runs west into the heart of Connacht. Along the edge of that road, where the tourists' maps turn brown and airy, in a small place called Rosmuc in Connemara, one can still visit Patrick Pearse's cottage, the summer holiday home of the schoolteacher-poet who championed the clandestine Irish Republican Brotherhood and was later executed for his part in the Easter Rising of

Below: Thatch used to be the universal roof covering for traditional Irish houses. However, over the years, as a result of modern farming methods – as well as a general lack of appreciation for its heritage value – thatch has become very scarce. Today, state grants and advice are helping to preserve those thatched cottages (approximately 2500) that survive nationwide, over 500 of which are found in Connacht. The roof of this particular cottage in the Aran Islands would have been made typically of rye straw and rope.

1916. One imagines he must have often sat inside the small windows dreaming his revolutionary dreams, and writing poetry which was perhaps sometimes a little on the maudlin side, an Irish trait.

From that place you can still see the unfettered sweep of the great, granite mountains, awesomely empty and clean, being casually stroked by suns that turn furze bushes into whorls of gold, and lakes into pools of molten silver; a scene that inspired Pearse to write these evocative lines:

> *The little fields where mountainy*
> *men have sown,*
> *And soon will reap,*
> *Close to the gates of Heaven.*

FROM: 'THE BEAUTY OF THIS WORLD' BY PATRICK PEARSE (1879–1916)

In 1649, when Oliver Cromwell came to Ireland, determined to bring the entire population to the Protestant faith, he once ordered the Irish natives to go 'to Hell or to Connacht . . .', to make room for his planters. Maybe he, too, got it right through happenstance. Many millions of visitors would, today, join with the natives in claiming that Connacht is so far away from Hell that it is, in the words of Pearse, as close as you can get on this earth to the gates of Heaven.

Below: The Currach *Boat-racing Competition is the highlight of* An Patrún, *'the Pattern', Festival which is held at the end of June on the island of Inishmore in honour of St Peter and St Paul's feast day. Three-man rowing teams come to Inishmore from all over Connemara and the nearby islands to compete. Ancient rowing skills and inherited strength are displayed by the participants and there is much cajoling and lively conversation as the observers cheer their favourite teams. Nowadays, too, the event has taken on a new spirit with a special women's event, allowing the 'fairer' sex to demonstrate their prowess on the sea.*

GALWAY
Cradle of the 'hidden Ireland'

GALWAY IS A COUNTY, is a city, is a state of mind. Galway is a republic within a republic; a principality of all the Irish pleasures; a dominion of dreams; a myth that is a rock-tipped reality; a myth upon which real purple heather grows; against whose shoreline the long Atlantic waves murmur mysteries.

Galway City and its great sweeping county hinterland is not just the capital of Connacht. It is also, in a spiritual way, the unchallenged capital of what people are now commonly terming the 'hidden Ireland'. Here, one of Europe's fastest growing cities has somehow contrived to marry the very best of modernity and economic development to all the worthwhile elements of a colourful history.

There are many areas of Ireland, especially towards the east coast, where one could argue that Europeanization has impacted heavily upon both the places and their people. Mainstream cultural and lifestyle changes are clearly evident at every level. The national media, largely headquartered in Dublin, today generally portrays the Irish as differing less and less from our European brethren. International lifestyle trends, for whatever commercial reason, are powerfully hyped, frequently adopted. And yet, against this background, the 'hidden Ireland' of which Galway is the capital continues to flourish.

In this world the old values still hold sway. Gaelic football and hurling are still far more popular than soccer, for example. Irish musicians and balladeers draw larger audiences than any others. In County Galway, in the Gaeltacht (Irish-speaking) region of south Connemara, not only is Irish the mother tongue for at least 40,000 people, it is also a live and vibrant element in the social intercourse of the city itself. In this world, people still go to church on Sundays; eat more potatoes than pasta; know their family trees, and folklore, and how to dance the old set dances. In

Left: Founded in 1812 by John D'Arcy, the twin-spired port of Clifden, 'the capital of Connemara', nestles where the mountains meet the Atlantic coast.

Above: Known as 'hookers', these heavy timber fishing boats with their tanned sails were also used to carry peat over the Aran Islands, which had no peat bogs of their own, at a time when peat provided the principal source of fuel.

all of Galway, both city and county, the 'hidden Ireland' is not hidden at all and this is probably the reason why the region so powerfully plays the heartstrings.

From each corner of Eyre Square, in the heart of Galway City, run four roads which all lead to some understanding of the Galway mystique. The road which runs north from Eyre Square, before swinging somewhat to the west, ends up hugging the shores of the lordly Corrib the great lake which meets the Atlantic near the ancient fishing village of the Claddagh. Further to the west is the town of Oughterard, which goes mad each May when the mayfly begin to rise and excite both the trout and the anglers. The Corrib hereabouts is at its most majestic. On its shores, quiet places like Conbur and Corrhanmona look over to horizons of drifting boats of anglers, blue skies, and peace.

The road that runs west from Eyre Square penetrates a totally different Galway. It runs again for about 60 miles (96 km) through some of Ireland's most strikingly rugged scenery, right through the heart of Connemara to Clifden. Connemara, under its sculpted weight of great mountains called The Twelve Pins, is as different from north and east Galway as chalk from cheese. Here, Gaelic is spoken to a man, and the people seem somehow smaller and quicker that their brethren towards the River Shannon. It is probably the difference between the fisherman and the farmer. Most Connemara men fish. To see their traditional boats, *currachs*, which they use the way farmers use tractors, dancing on the sea, is to observe artistry. Their ancestors needed to be quick and hardy to eke out a living between seas and rocks and harder places. Times are easier now with the explosion of new industries, such as aquaculture, but Connemara remains a law unto itself. Despite heavy penalties, they still make *poitín* by the gallon here, especially at Christmas. The colourless, fiery moonshine, distilled in quiet glens or on remote offshore islands, tastes of bog and heather, a little of Heaven and a little of Hell.

The three Aran Islands, Inishmore, Inishmaan and Inisheer, which groan under the weight of tourists all year round, are like fragments of Connemara flung offshore. Dun Aenghus, mysterious clifftop fort on Inishmore, the largest of the three, is awe-inspiring. Inisheer, closer to the Clare coast, is the most serene.

The road south from Eyre Square runs through another world again. Past the village of Oranmore, heading towards Clare and Limerick, it runs through oyster country; through hunting country; through green fields and tall trees. Villages like Oranmore, Clarinbridge and Kilcolgan all lie inshore from the world-famous oyster beds of Galway Bay. Each autumn, when the oysters are in season, a jetsetters' Oyster Festival in Galway City attracts scores of revellers.

The infectious passion with which Galwegians play is reflected in another way in many areas along the road which runs east. En route to the shore of the River Shannon, it passes between the towns of Tuam and sprawling Loughrea where, Sunday after Sunday, great games of Gaelic football and hurling are played with rare fire, skill and competitiveness. Once, in the 1960s, the Tuam football team won the All-Ireland Championship three years in a row, a most difficult feat. The players who accomplished this triple triumph, now in their fifties, are still regarded almost as demigods by the young boys and men who can be seen practising and honing their skills in the playing fields along the roadside.

The strong market town of Ballinasloe, in the heart of the west's horse country, reveals another element of the real Galway. Here, at the beginning of each October, is staged what is now Europe's largest

Below: Fishermen pulling their currach *up on the beach. These sturdy, hawk-prowed craft, traditionally made from tarred canvas stretched over a timber frame, have been used for fishing off the coast of Galway for many centuries. Today, in spite of increasing industrialization, the economy of much of the coastal region of Connacht continues to rely heavily on fishing for its social and economic development.*

Above: A poitín *raid. The penalty for possession of this illegal liquor is severe.*

Left: Prized for their agility, the origins of the Connemara pony go back 2500 years to when Celtic warriors brought horses to Ireland to draw war chariots.

traditional horse fair. On the first Monday of the month, Ballinasloe's great amphitheatre, Fair Green, is swamped by thousands of horses. Many of them are the horses of Ireland's travelling people who, from dawn until dusk, can be seen riding furiously bareback up and down through the thick of the action. Deals involving dozens of horses are going on everywhere. There is back-slapping, hand-slapping; all the tricks of buying and selling. There are trick-o-the-loop men slipping through the crowds like ghosts, fortune-tellers, three-card-trick men. Usually, on the fringes of the fair, the strong men among the travellers engage in bareknuckle fisticuffs in prearranged bouts to determine, in effect, who is the 'king of the tinkers'. Two centuries ago, so great was the reputation of the Ballinasloe Fair that the purchasing officers for the armies of the Czar of Russia used to come here to buy their cavalry mounts.

For one of the finest examples of the Galway spirit, one should follow the road east to Ballybrit, just off the edge of the city, where, at the end of July, the Galway Races are held for an entire week. The Galway Races are different from any other race meeting in Ireland. It is significant that many tens of thousands of visitors who come to Galway for Race Week never go to the track at all; never bet on a horse. They come for the almost feverish merrymaking which is the climax of the region's summer tourist season. More champagne is drunk in Galway during that week than anywhere else in Ireland. There are more high jinks, more card games for incredibly high stakes, more street fun for the masses. The skies are full of private helicopters heading to and from the track in a spending spree worth at least £20 million to all the local tills. Each year the total betting take is higher than ever before. This happens even during periods of economic downturn! Galway Races, fabled in song and story, are an experience for all the senses. Only Galway could stage them.

LEITRIM

The Cinderella county

CLICHÉS ARE OFTEN VERY APT. They call Leitrim 'the Cinderella county' and you would not find a better description. She is a waifish scrap of a thing, tiny, with a smudged nose and a crystal slipper that glitters at the waterfall of Glencar. She has even got her very own Garden of Eden!

It is outside Rossinver. Here, there has always been a townland called Eden. A gentle Englishman called Rod Alston visited Eden 20 years ago. He saw a cottage there, empty, as were many by emigration. It even had an apple tree, although it lay on its side beside the cottage, its roots drying and dying inside a thin uprooted sod. Alston bought the cottage and almost the first thing he did was to right the tree, stake it and then feed its famished roots. Today it brings forth good fruit and surrounding it is one of the west of Ireland's best organic gardens. The story of this garden of Eden is in many respects the story of Leitrim.

The west, economically, is the poorest region in Ireland. Leitrim is the poorest county in the west. Her drumlin soil is acidic and thin. Her winters can be harsh, wet, windy. In the 1950s and 1960s her population was so ravaged by emigration that it was reduced to below 30,000. At one time there were even doubts about whether the county could survive as a viable unit.

Just as in the Cinderella story, help came from outside – one hesitates to say from 'a fairy godfather' – but in the shape of a man with imagination. His name was John McGivern, otherwise known as Johnny Macaroni. He came back from America in the darkest days of the early 1950s, and in the small village of Glenfarne he built the 'Ballroom of Romance', a dance hall to which he brought the biggest dance bands in all of Ireland. Thereafter, every Sunday night, without fail, the dapper, tuxedoed, Italian-shod McGivern went onstage, turned the lights low, and sang, 'Have You Ever Been Lonely?'. Then, as the band played softly,

Left: Gaelic football is a game which combines aspects of soccer and rugby. Here, Leitrim play Galway in the first round of the All-Ireland Championships.

169

he encouraged Leitrim boy and Leitrim girl, dancing shyly together, perhaps for the first time, to exchange names and perhaps peck each other on the cheek if they felt bold enough. McGivern called it the 'Romantic Interlude', and it was a major attraction, especially for tongue-tied young men. Years later, before William Trevor wrote his classic short story, *The Ballroom of Romance*, John McGivern, who died recently, had statistics to show that his ballroom, a blazing bright light on a darkly drumlin horizon, had indeed created hundreds of marriages.

Today, there are many bright nightspots and clubs to visit in prospering towns like Carrick-on-Shannon and Mohill and Manorhamilton and Ballinamore. Maybe the best index to the new vitality of a county once threatened with extinction is the fact that its Gaelic footballers recently won the Connacht Championships and made a gallant attempt to win the All-Ireland title. Nothing so sharply defines the county's identity and pride. Yet there is something poignant, too, in all the subcurrents of modern Leitrim. So much hurting by the past generations; so much poverty then; so many tens of thousands of enforced emigrants, all mean that, even in the midst of summertime gaiety, the strong folk memory of loss and regret is never too far away. It is neither intrusive nor depressing – rather the opposite nowadays – but it is there. The setting sun that X-rays the breathtaking valleys clearly exposes the shadows of the potato ridges and furrows of the past. Crops grew here to feed thousands whose crumbling gables testify to eventual defeat. When the potato crop failed during the Great Famine of 150 years ago (1845–49), few areas suffered

Below: Rod Alston in his 'Garden of Eden' which is situated in Leitrim's drumlin country. Over the last 20 years, he has transformed the 21-acre plot from 'a chaos of thorn and bramble' into 'a garden that is both productive and beautiful'.

more. In a Leitrim pub there comes a special silence when someone sings any of the many emigration songs that recall the era:

> *I am bidding them all farewell,*
> *With an aching heart I will bid them adieu,*
> *For tomorrow I sail far away,*
> *All across the wild foam, for to seek a new home*
> *On the Shores of Amerikay.*

However, in Leitrim that mood will not last long. No sooner will the echoes of the song have died away than some fluter or fiddler will strike up a lively tune and, before the night is over, the visitor is likely to be told in detail of how the abused tenantry of this region at last ended the allegedly cruel career of the county's most hated landlord of the last century.

When Lord Leitrim of Mohill was murdered in 1878 in nearby County Donegal, where he also owned huge estates, the police thought they had a clear clue to the identity of one of his murderers because, in the dead lord's fist, they found a 'clump' of red hair which he had torn from the head of one of his assailants. However, when they went to investigate, they found that every redheaded male within 70 miles (112 km) had willingly undergone a similar semi-scalping experience. Today the great Lough Rynn House near Mohill, from which the autocratic lord once ruled over 90,000 acres (36,423 ha) in four counties, is one of the area's premier tourist attractions.

Survival was always the name of the game in Leitrim. Even in modern times the people are ultra-sensitive about the integrity of their identity. They react sharply, usually en masse, to any media criticism of their own place. They strongly dislike the political reality that, for voting purposes, their beloved county is annexed to neighbouring Sligo. There is also continuing opposition to forestry developments in the county which springs largely from a fierce wish not to surrender farmland to trees.

Above: Emigrants at the Quayside (The Illustrated London News). The mass exodus from Ireland that took place during the Great Famine (1845–49) represented the pinnacle of a wave of emigration that started at the beginning of the 19th century and continued right up until the 1980s. Between 1845 and 1936 the population was reduced from over eight million to a mere four and a half million. The unique decline of Ireland's population during this period affected all classes, religions and regions, although the intensity of overseas movement was greatest from the poorer counties on Ireland's western seaboard. It is now estimated that 70 million members of the Irish diaspora are scattered throughout the world. An estimated 40 million of these live in the United States alone.

MAYO

A sacred 'queendom'

THE THIRD LARGEST COUNTY is not pronounced 'mayo' at all in the local dialect. It is infinitely more of a 'mmayOO' sound, softly and proudly articulated. That final vowel rides as high and airy above the rest as the holy mountain of Croagh Patrick soars above the animated picture postcard that is the town of Westport on the surf line of Clew Bay.

Hunched slightly forward over the town, the summit almost always cloud-wreathed, the holy mountain has the profile of a shawled matriarch kneeling in prayer before a smoking turf fire. It looks formidable, somehow indomitable, yet calm, like a seashore grandmother scanning the bay for the first sight of the family fishing boat beating for home, an appropriate metaphor, as it happens, for a county where formidable females have left an indelible imprint on both the past and present.

There is a great national pilgrimage to Croagh Patrick on the final Sunday of July, known as Reek Sunday. Up to 100,000 pilgrims climb to the summit – an awesome sight – to hear Mass and receive Holy Communion in a grey little oratory up in the mists. The climbs used to take place at night, the pilgrims' torches creating a writhing golden-skinned 235 foot (72 m) serpent; the only one St Patrick never banished from Ireland. In those years the local people employed a herd of donkeys to ferry supplies of tea and soft drinks to canvas-roofed bothies along the way and on the summit itself. I once paid five old shillings (now 25 pence), then a huge price, for a single cup of tea, to a feisty local woman who justified the price by saying she had climbed the mountain four times in the previous two days to bring up supplies. Outside, as I drank the best tea I've ever tasted, stalwarts like her, many in bleeding bare feet, toiled towards the clouds. Faith, it seems, *can* move mountains; the centuries-old pilgrims' path is constantly being eroded and broken down by the tens of thousands of feet.

Left: Looking out from Clew Bay to Clare Island, the family seat of the 16th century 'Queen of the West', Grace O'Malley.

In the nearby village of Knock an event took place in 1879 which would have a profound effect on the county of Mayo. Here, on a warm August evening, 15 local people claimed to have seen an apparition of the Blessed Virgin Mary on the outside gable wall of the local chapel. Today, in consequence, Knock is Ireland's leading pilgrimage centre – 1.5 million pilgrims visit the village annually – and numerous miracles are claimed to have occurred there. The village also now has the country's largest church – Our Lady's Basilica – which can accommodate 20,000 people and often needs to. Even cynics are impressed by a very special serene atmosphere surrounding this gentle place.

On all the roads that lead to Knock, everywhere in the county, the scores of Marian shrines and roadside grottos are the best maintained in Ireland. Around almost every bend, in robes of blue and white, the Lady of Mayo is to be seen surrounded by flowers and homage. Her moulded features, rendered hereabouts as Celtic and serene, but with a powerful directness about them, never fail to remind me of drawings of the other great lady who once ruled this mountain matriarchy, the warrior queen Grace O'Malley, commonly known as Granuaile.

Beautiful, wild, wily, passionate Grace O'Malley, the queen of all the seas around Clew Bay; a pirate queen; a female free-booter in a totally male-dominated era. The Mayo historian, Anne Chambers, has written a splendid history of her lifetime achievements and daring exploits in the years from about 1550 to 1600. I love the image of Granuaile, at the prime of her powers, sailing proudly up the mouth of the River Thames to London in her own fierce warship to meet with Queen Elizabeth in the

Above: Ireland's President, Mary Robinson, who took office in 1990.

Left and below: The fine east window of the Murrisk Augustinian Friary which was founded in 1457. Beautifully situated by Clew Bay, this is traditionally the starting point for pilgrims climbing Croagh Patrick.

Elizabethan court on equal terms. The 'virgin' queen is said to have been fascinated and hugely impressed by her, as well she might. Today, on striking Clare Island, off the Mayo coast, the remains of one of her castles, cliff-perched still, after all these centuries, seem to echo with her powerful presence.

Perhaps because of the early power of Granuaile, County Mayo, even more than the other western counties, has the heft of a matriarchy about it even now. In most agricultural societies with a Catholic tradition and large families, mothers played a vital role, and the women of Mayo, who have always been noted for their thrift, energy, and enterprise, are no exception. There is a common saying often used to illustrate the shrewdness and vitality of Mayo's mothers: 'She would mind mice at a crossroads!'

The first woman President of Ireland, Mary Robinson (still gracefully in office at the time of writing), is in many ways the Granuaile of her era. Already an internationally-famed constitutional lawyer and feminist before she was proposed for the state's highest office, the Ballina woman was not expected to win. But she sailed forth against all the odds and won over the people of Ireland in a decisive election victory. Since then, with intellect, with elegance, and with a forceful kind of compassion for all humanity which has seen her catapulted onto the international scene, President Robinson has enhanced both the office which she holds, and, in the wider context, the entire proud reputation of Mayo matriarchs. A welcoming light burns always in the window of the presidential palace in Dublin; a token of the welcoming lights that have always been burning in Mayo's windows for the homecomings of generations of both seasonal and long-term emigrants.

It is said that although 400 people died in a dreadful famine march along the shoreline of Doo Lough (Louisburgh) in 1847 – they were seeking food from workhouse authorities – many more would have died had it not been for the womenfolk among them. It was they who drove the survivors on.

Right: The annual 'farmers' race' on the beach in Louisburgh in County Mayo.

Below: Céide Fields, a megalithic site containing tombs and dwellings, dating from the Stone and Bronze Ages that have been excavated in northern Mayo.

ROSCOMMON

Evoking the ancient

O**N A MIDSUMMER EVENING** a dying sun illuminates Rathcroghan, in the green heart of County Roscommon. This ancient stone, which seems to grow much taller than its six feet (2 m) in the lowering light, is said to mark the tomb of the fierce King Dathi, the last pagan ruler of Ireland. Beyond it are *Relig na Ri*, *Rath na Tarbh* and *Rathbeg*, just some of the seemingly endless megalithic tombs of those rulers who preceded Dathi, including Maeve, the legendary Queen of Connacht who also ruled and loved in this place in the days before St Patrick.

There is a general view that Roscommon's colourful present tends to be over-shadowed by her exotic past. Certainly, the county's past and present are fused in a compelling way not matched anywhere else even in the west of Ireland. Barely a month passes when the scuba divers, fishermen and boatmen who ply the ever-busier Shannon, bordering the county to the east, do not find artefacts that evoke the centuries: stone axes, bone buttons, coins, the heavy pikes of the wars and rebellions.

In Lough Gara, off the road between Boyle and Ballaghaderreen, the lowering of the water level 30 years ago recently revealed 400 drowned crannogs (lake dwellings), hitherto unknown. Nearby were the well-preserved remains of their fleet of 40 dug-out canoes.

Likewise the county's green acres are fairly littered with historic memorabilia. Ogulla Well is here, in the shade both of a bloodstained O'Conor Castle and a broken Dominican priory, veined now with ivy and the clawings of centuries. It was in this place that St Patrick is said to have baptized the daughters of the High King of Ireland, Eithne and Fidelma, thereby ensuring the success of his Christianizing of the paganlands. He did it under the raised eyebrows of another of those pagan hills, Carnfree, where the kings of Connacht are thought to have been crowned.

Clonalis House, outside Castlerea in the west of the county, typifies the

Left: A county of rolling hills, peat bogs and low mountains, Roscommon is traditionally a sheep rearing region.

Right: Turlough Carolan (1670–1738) was a blind harpist who travelled the west of Ireland and the midlands, playing music for Roman Catholic and Protestant patrons. Having diligently avoided either political or religious controversy in his lyrics, he was able to forge links between planters and Gaels, both of whom, rich and poor alike, attended his funeral in their thousands. However, following his death – and in the face of the increasing English pressure that was exerted on Ireland during the 17th century – the harp, the ancient symbol of Ireland, lost popularity among Ireland's 'well to do', becoming an increasingly down-market instrument, played more often by beggars.

Below: Ogulla Well, in County Roscommon, whose waters are said to provide a cure for ailments of the eyes.

sheer height and width of Roscommon's history. It is the ancestral home of the Clan O'Conor, a family which produced no less than 11 high kings of Ireland and 24 kings of Connacht. Today it houses a rich display of artefacts, including the harp of Blind O'Carolan, the greatest of the Irish harpists whose compositions reputedly include the music for 'The Star Spangled Banner'. There, too, one can learn the well-documented story of 'Lady Betty', a convicted murderer, who had her sentence commuted on condition that she carried out the hangman's grisly duties without any fee. The gaol, in which it is said she enjoyed her work, still stands, a mighty stone building in the centre of the town. In Fuerty graveyard lies another of Connacht's anti-heros, Robert Ormsby, known as *Riobard na nGligearnacht*, 'Robert of the Jingling Harness' who is remembered darkly in the local folklore for his many cruelties towards his tenants in the Cromwellian era.

All of this co-exists with a vivacious modern way of living. The pubs in the main Roscommon towns are second only to some of the country pubs for their nightlife and the quality of the music. More often than not the visitor is likely to hear at least one of the famous bitter-sweet songs of the satirical troubadour, Percy French:

> *You remember young Peter O'Loughlin, of course,*
> *Well, here he is here at the head of the Force.*
> *I met him to-day, I was crossing the Strand,*
> *And he stopped the whole street wid wan wave of his hand;*
> *And there we stood talking of days that are gone,*
> *While the whole population of London looked on,*
> *But for all these great powers he's wishful, like me,*
> *To be back where dark Mourne sweeps down to the sea.*

FROM: 'THE MOUNTAINS O'MOURNE' BY PERCY FRENCH (1854–1919)

He had a fine way with words, the Strokestown man. So, too, have his fellow countymen and women. I gave one a seat in my car recently near a somnolently serene Lough Gara. I asked what the fishing was like. The answer was immediate: 'The best fishing is to be found around those signs that say "No fishing"!'

There is a castle outside Roscommon town called Donamon Castle. Curving like a sickle around the River Suck, this site has been fortified since 1154. It was then the powerhouse of the ferocious O'Finaghty family who owned all the lands they could see from their highest windows in all directions.

Today it is a seminary for a gentle order of priests called The Divine Word Missionaries. I heard them singing a Mass here once, the shadows of their chapel almost visibly tenanted with the gentled spirits of old warriors, princes, kings. The silent river seemed to take the music away with it on its eddies and currents, as it flowed past other old ruined monasteries and castles, passage graves, and burial mounds; flowed over the hidden bronze daggers and rusted spears and pikes, past the holy wells and unholy hanging places. At some point on its journey it passed the extended shadow of that still-living tombstone of the last of the pagan kings of this county and of all the kings there ever were.

Below: The Rathcroghan Stone, or Cruachain, has great significance in Irish mythology – and literature – for marking the spot when the kings of Connacht are thought to have been crowned. It is mentioned in the Gaelic legends as the capital of Ailill MacMata, husband of Maeve, (who is herself thought to be buried here). The site also has great religious significance since it contains the cairn, Oweynagat 'the Cave of the Cats', the legendary gateway to the Other World.

SLIGO

County of poets and painters

I MET A MERRY, unpublished poet in the city of Sligo. He was 60 years old and there was the froth of a pint of Guinness on his upper lip when he uttered a few of his lines:

> *The working men of Sligo,*
> *Don't care a damn for Yeats,*
> *All we want are pints of porter,*
> *Spuds and bacon on our plates!*

This happy poet's name was Melody, an appropriate surname for a bright spark of Sligo's soul. He was one of the many thousands of ex-soldiers that the garrison town of Sligo has given to the armies of the world down the centuries. In his case the army was the US Army and his war was the Korean War.

I contrast those eyes that were still so bright and lively with the gloomy and foreboding epitaph etched on the gravestone of the more famous poet, W. B. Yeats, a few miles out on the road in Drumcliff cemetery.

> *Cast a cold Eye*
> *On Life on Death*
> *Horseman pass by!*

The real ethos of County Sligo, as I have known and experienced it for more than 30 years, was infinitely better captured by the 'unknown soldier' who laughed at life than by the poet laureate whose dark and essentially tormented presence still hangs over Sligo as distinctively as the silvered forelock hung over his own forehead; as lonely Benbulben Mountain looms over Sligo town.

Left: William Butler Yeats is buried at the foot of Benbulben which rises majestically out of the north Sligo plain to a height of 1725 feet (526 m).

Sligo is often known as 'Yeats Country', an accolade which at one level his powerful literary genius deserves. Also it is good for tourism. But at a deeper level it is a flawed attribution in many ways. The real and very earthy Sligo never belonged to William Butler Yeats any more than he belonged to it. He was actually born in Dublin and spent the greater part of his childhood in London. The Sligo that impacted most upon him was the Sligo of the visitor, and a relatively privileged one at that.

Indeed I would claim that his brother, Jack Yeats, the painter, whose work is increasingly in vogue nowadays, could properly lay more claim to the tribute. Jack Yeats' paintings of popular Sligo events, like fair days and horse races, do catch the soul of this county. His faces, animated and at ease with themselves, are the kind of faces one still sees on the streets of Ballymote and Tobercurry; in the fields around Gurteen; walking the golden sands of Strandhill. They are real. You can shake their hands and they will smile at you. William's strange people seem tenanted more to the superstitious county of his genius that to the county of which he was so fond.

Recently, while visiting Drumcliff cemetery, I watched a fiery farmyard rooster, the picture of a primitive kind of vitality, fly up onto one of the tombstones, sadly not that of Yeats, where he cock-a-doodle-dooed for the whole wide world. That's my Sligo.

For those that seek tombland and ancient castles, archaeology, history,

Above: W. B. Yeats (1865–1939) died in the south of France in 1939, and it was not until 1948 that he was finally laid to rest in Drumcliff by the Protestant church where his grandfather had been rector. He wrote his own epitaph.

Right: The Yeats brothers spent many holidays in Ballisodare and Sligo town with their maternal grandparents. Here, Gaelic legends provided much of the inspiration for W. B. Yeats' early poetry. He won the Nobel Prize in 1923 and his outstanding contribution to literature is commemorated by this sculpture by Rohan Gillespie which sits in Sligo town.

Left: An untitled painting by Jack Yeats (1871–1957), Ireland's greatest modern painter, displays his ability to capture the vernacular of his beloved Sligo at its most colourful and vigorous.

echoes of centuries, they are all here. There are books galore that will tell you all about the misted and essentially heartbreaking Celtic legends attached to the empurpled mountains and caverns of Sligo. Go south to the Strand of Streedagh and you can still almost hear the grinding noise of the waterlogged Spanish Armada foundering here.

But Sligo people, though well-versed in the richness of their own history, and proud of it too, are more likely to get a bright light in their eyes at the mention of Michael Coleman than at the mention of either the poet or the slaughtered Spaniards. Coleman, an accomplished and truly lively fiddler, evocative of the local spirit, emigrated to the United States and began a brilliant recording career there 60 years ago. His records, in that era and beyond, were as popular as those of the golden Athlone tenor, Count John McCormack. Coleman is still one of the father figures of Irish traditional music and thanks to his influence, Sligo continues to have a spirited corps of musicians who manage very sucessfully to 'make the timber talk'.

When I think of Sligo I think of good nights in good company; of exciting modern theatre by companies like the Hawk's Well group in the city; of children singing and dancing and playing at the Sligo Feis (competitive festival); of the awesome beauty of Easkey, south of Sligo, whose very name is an amalgam of the words 'sea' and 'sky'. I think of Gurteen and the prized racing greyhounds, and of Enniscrone, where the salty baths, they say, would bring a dead man to life, if you could get him immersed in them quickly enough. And I think of the fabled Coney Island, after which it is claimed the New York counterpart is named. It is off the road between Sligo and the resort of Strandhill. At low tide, with care and local advice, you can drive across golden strands out to an island of gentle wonder and serenity.

There is another special place along the Sligo coastline. It is near the now empty little town of Aughris, ruined by emigration. It is called *Coragh Dtonn*. The Gaelic name springs from the fact that the cliff hereabouts is concave. The sea, in its green, heaves against it, especially on summer nights, producing an eerie sound which is unforgettable, but, somehow, not sad. It sounds a bit like a tumult of ancient warriors celebrating a battle long ago; a battle won rather than lost. It is elemental, exciting, enchanting. It is the growl of life in Sligo's throat.

Below: Tradition along the west coast holds that the practice of bathing in hot water and seaweed – which contains high concentrations of iodine – provides relief from the painful symptoms of rheumatism and arthritis.

Left: The lofty Benbo Mountain, which sweeps to a height of 1361 feet (415 m) on the approach to Sligo, south of Manorhamilton in Leitrim, is a typical feature in a monumental landscape often referred to as 'Yeats country'.

BIBLIOGRAPHY

Bardon, Jonathan, *A History of Ulster*. Belfast, The Blackstaff Press, 1992.

Birr Castle, Visitors' Book.

Brett, C. E. B., *Buildings of Belfast 1700–1914*. Belfast, Friar's Bush Press, 1985.

Brett, David, *The Construction of Heritage*. Cork University Press, 1996.

Caldicott, C. E. J., Gough, H. and Pitton, J. J., *The Huguenots and Ireland – Anatomy of an Emigration*. Dun Laoghaire, The Glendale Press, 1987.

Craig, Maurice, *Dublin 1660–1860*. London, Penguin, 1992.

Deane, J. A. K., *The Gate Lodges of Ulster*. Belfast, Ulster Architechtural Heritage Society, 1994.

Deane, Seamus, *The Field Day Anthology of Irish Writing*. Derry, Field Day Publication, 1991.

Delaney, Ruth, *Ireland's Inland Waterways*. Belfast, Appletree Press, 1992.

Encyclopædia Britannica. Encyclopædia Britannica Inc., 1978.

Evans, E. Estyn, *Irish Folk Ways*. London, Routledge Kegan & Paul, 1957.

Evans, Rosemary, *The Visitor's Guide to Northern Ireland*. Derbyshire, Moorland Publishing, 1987.

The Everyman Guide to Ireland. Paris, *Editions Nouveaux-Loisirs* (a subsidiary of *Gallimard*), 1994.

Flanagan, Deirdre and Laurence, *Irish Place Names*. Dublin, Gill & Macmillan, 1992.

Flower, R., *The Irish Tradition*. Oxford, Clarendon Press, 1947.

Foster, R.F. (edited by), *The Oxford Illustrated History of Ireland*. Oxford University Press, 1989.

Galloway, Peter, *The Cathedrals of Ireland*. Belfast, Institute of Irish Studies, 1992.

Gregory, Augusta, Lady, *Complete Irish Mythology*. London, Reed Consumer Books, 1994.

Harbinson, Peter, *Guide to National and Historic Monuments of Ireland*. Dublin, Gill & Macmillan, 1992.

Heaney, Seamus, *Death of a Naturalist*. London, Faber & Faber, 1966.

Heaney, Seamus, *Station Island*. London, Faber & Faber, 1984.

Hickey, Helen, *Images of Stone*. Belfast, The Blackstaff Press, 1976.

Hill, Ian, *The Fish of Ireland*. Belfast, Appletree Press, 1992.

Hill, Christopher and Ian, *The North*. Belfast, Blackstaff Press, 1995.

Hill, Ian with Blair, Robert and Kirk, Bill, *Northern Ireland*. Belfast, Blackstaff Press, 1986.

Hill, Ian and Megaher, Paddy, *Ireland Guide*. Dublin, *Bord Fáilte*/Gill & Macmillan, 1993.

The Insight Guide to Ireland. HongKong, APA Publications, 1992.

Kee, Robert, *Ireland, a History*. Revised and updated by Robert Kee, Great Britain, Weidenfeld & Nicolson, 1980.

Killanin, Lord and Duignan, Michael V., *The Shell Guide to Ireland*. Revised and updated by Peter Harbinson, Dublin, Gill & Macmillan, 1989.

Livingstone, Peadar, *The Fermanagh Story*. Enniskillen, *Cumann Seanchais Chlochair*, 1969.

Macafee, Dr I. C., *A Concise Ulster Dictionary*. Oxford University Press, 1996.

McGahern, John, *Amongst Women*. London, Faber & Faber, 1990.

McMinn, Joseph, *Jonathan's Travels – Swift in Ireland*. Belfast, Appletree Press, 1994.

Moore, Patrick, *The Astonomy of Birr Castle*. London, Mitchell Beazley, 1971.

Nelson, Charles E. and Walsh, Wendy F., *Trees of Ireland*. Dublin, Lilliput Press, 1993.

Newman, Kate, *Dictionary of Ulster Biography*. Belfast, Institute of Irish Studies, 1993.

O'Donnell, E. E., *The Annals of Dublin*. Dublin, Wolfhound Press, 1987.

O'Faolain, Eileen, *Children of the Salmon and Other Irish Folk Tales*. Swords, Poolbeg Press, 1988.

Regional Tourist Board Guides for all 26 counties contained with the Republic of Ireland.

Rogers, Mary, *Prospect of Erne*. Enniskillen, Water Gate Press, 1971.

Sandford, Ernest, *Discover Northern Ireland*. Belfast, Northern Ireland Tourist Board, 1976.

Welch, Robert, *The Oxford Companion Guide to Architecture in Ireland 1837–1921*. Dublin, Irish Academic Press, 1994.

Whilde, A., *Irish Red Data Book 2: Vertebrates*. Belfast, HMSO, 1993.

Williams, Guy St J. and Hyland, Francis P. M., *The Irish Derby*. London, J. A. Allen, 1980.

Williams, Jeremy, *A Companion Guide to Architecture in Ireland 1837–1921*. Dublin, Irish Academic Press, 1994.

INDEX

PICTURE CREDITS

Acknowledgements

The publishers are very grateful to Pat Maclean from the Ulster Museum in Belfast for her unswerving help, as well as staff from tourist information offices throughout Ireland, especially Margaret Duffy, Nuala Kenna and Michael O'Keeffe from *Bord Fáilte* in Dublin.

Additional thanks are offered to the following: Rod Alston from Eden Plants; Eugene Archer and Richard Collins from BirdWatch Ireland; Don Cotton; Louise Delahunty from The Curragh Racecourse; Christine McIvor from the Ulster American Folkpark; Caroline O'Brien from Goff's Bloodstock Sales; Barry O'Reilly from the Office of Public Works, Dublin; and Chris Wilson from the Wexford Wildfowl Reserve.

The following poems have been reproduced with the permission of the publishers: **45:** reprinted by kind permission of Farrar, Straus & Giroux, Inc. excerpts from 'Act of Union' from *Poems 1965–1975* by Seamus Heaney. Copyright © Seamus Heaney; **88:** excerpts from 'Shancoduff' reproduced by kind permission of the Trustees of the Estate of Patrick Kavanagh c/o Peter Fallon, Literary Agent, Loughcrew, Oldcastle, County Meath, Ireland.

Picture Credits
Cover: Tony Stone Images, Joe Cornish ref A294D 297574-002R; half-title: T. Kelly; 9: J. Marffy © Salamander Books Ltd; 10-11: The Slide File, ref: LB 1339D/2; 12: R. Mills; 13: The Slide File, ref: COLB 393; 14-15: R. Mills; 16 (left & right): R. Mills; 17 (above) The Slide File, ref: KWX 315; 17 (below): The Slide File, ref: LB 1433B NR; 18-19: T. Kelly; 20-21: The Slide File, ref: DS 52 NR; 22 (above): R. Mills; 22 (below): G.A. Duncan, ref: P775; 23: R. Mills; 24-25: R. Mills; 26-27: R. Mills; 28 (above): R. Mills; 28 (below): The Cork Examiner, ref: 297 G; 29: The Slide File, ref: LB 1674; 30-31: R. Mills; page 32: The Slide File, ref: CMC 271; 33 (above): R. Mills; 33 (left) The Slide File, ref: AN 466; 34-35: M. Tarry; 36 (right): R. Mills; 36 (below): photograph reproduced courtesy of the National Library of Ireland, ref: 15694; 37: The Slide File, ref: COLB 343B/2; 38-39: R. Mills; 40: The Slide File, ref: XTH 463/1; 41 (above): R. Mills; 41 (below): T. Murphy; 42-43: G. Sweeney; 44: photograph reproduced with the kind permission of the Trustees of the Ulster Museum Belfast; 45: G. Sweeney; 46-47: The Slide File, ref: HILL 1062; 48 (above): photograph reproduced with the kind permission of the Trustees of the Ulster Museum Belfast; 48 (below): photograph reproduced with the kind permission of the Trustees of the Ulster Museum Belfast; 49: The Slide File, ref: FD 13/2; 50-51: The Slide File, ref: HILL 664/1; 52: The Slide File, ref: HILL 312/2; 53: G. Sweeney; 54-55: painting reproduced with the kind permission of the Trustees of the Ulster Museum Belfast © Mrs J. Donnelly; 55 (above): The Slide File, ref: AN 251; 56-57: The Slide File, ref: HILL 940 NR; 58: The Slide File, ref: HILL 802C; 59: G. Sweeney; 60 (below): photograph reproduced with the kind permission of the Trustees of the Ulster Museum Belfast; 60-61: The Slide File, ref: JBT 60; 61(below): photograph reproduced with the kind permission of the Trustees of the Ulster Museum Belfast; 62-63: R. Mills; 64 (above): photograph reproduced with the kind permission of the Trustees of the Ulster Museum Belfast; 64 (below): G. Sweeney; 65: G. Sweeney; 66-67: G. Sweeney; 68-69: photograph reproduced with the kind permission of the Trustees of the Ulster Museum Belfast; 69 (above): The Slide File, ref: RAMS 107; 70 (above): G. Sweeney; 70-71: G.Sweeney; 72-73: The Slide File, ref: POAG 71; 74-75: G. Sweeney; 76 (above): G. Sweeney; 76 (below): G. Sweeney; 77: G. Sweeney; 78-79: G. Sweeney; 80 (below): painting reproduced with the kind permission of the Trustees of the Ulster Museum Belfast © Mrs J. Donnelly; 80-81: G. Sweeney; 82-83: The Slide File, ref: JJB 3984; 84: T. Kelly; 85: The Slide File, ref: JJB 3990A; 86-87: G. Sweeney; 88 (above): The Slide File, ref: JJB 3301B; 88 (below): The Slide File, ref: GEM 3654; 89: R. Mills; 90-91: The Slide File, ref: HILL 274; 92: Corbis-Bettmann, ref: E420; 93: photograph reproduced with kind permission of the Ulster American Folk Park; 94-95: T. Kelly; 96 (above): Hulton Deutsch, ref: P24969; 96 (below): photograph reproduced with the kind permission of the Trustees of the Ulster Museum Belfast; 97: T. Kelly; 98-99: T. Kelly; 100: T. Kelly; 101: T. Kelly; 102-103: T. Kelly; 104: T. Kelly; 105 (above): T. Kelly; 105 (below): Mary Evans Picture Library, ref: 979901; 106-107: T. Kelly; 108-109: T. Kelly; 110-111: T. Kelly; 112: T. Kelly; 113: photograph reproduced with the kind permission of The Curragh Racecourse; 114-115: T. Kelly; 116 (above): T. Kelly; 116 (below): T. Kelly; 117: T. Kelly; 118-119: T. Kelly; 120: T. Kelly; 121 (above): Mary Evans Picture Library, ref: 979927; 121 (below): T. Kelly; 122-123: T. Kelly; 124: T. Kelly; 125: Mary Evans Picture Library, ref: 979902; 126-127:T. Kelly; 128: T. Kelly; 129: Mary Evans Picture Library, ref: 979905; 130-131: T. Kelly; 132: Mary Evans Picture Library, ref: 979930; 133: T. Kelly; 134-135: T. Kelly; 135 (above): T. Kelly; 136-137: T. Kelly; 138-139: T. Kelly; 140: *The Illustrated London News*, ref: ILN 19 Apr 1845 p253; 141: T. Kelly; 142-143: T. Kelly; 144: photographs reproduced with the kind permission of MacCormack's Studios, Athlone; 145: T. Kelly; 146-147: T. Kelly; 148: Mary Evans Picture Library, ref: 979931; 149: T. Kelly; 150-151: T. Kelly; 152-153: T. Kelly; 154 (above): Mary Evans Picture Library, ref: 979906; 155: T. Kelly; 156-157: T. Kelly; 158-159: C. Doyle; 160: C. Doyle; 161: C. Doyle; 162-163: T. Kelly; 164: C. Doyle; 165: C. Doyle; 166-167: T. Kelly; 167 (above): C. Doyle; 168-169: C. Doyle; 170: C. Doyle; 171: photograph reproduced with the kind permission of the Trustees of the Ulster Museum Belfast; 172-173: T. Kelly; 174: T. Kelly; 175 (above): photograph reproduced with the kind permission of *Áras an Uachtaráin;* 175: C. Doyle; 176 (below): T. Kelly; 176-177: C. Doyle; 178-179: T. Kelly; 180 (above): Hulton Getty, ref: P58396; 180 (below): T. Kelly; 181: T. Kelly; 182-183: T. Kelly; 184 (above): T. Kelly; 184 (below): T. Kelly; 185 (above): photograph reproduced with the kind permission of the Trustees of the Ulster Museum Belfast © Anne and Michael Yeats; 185 (below): T. Kelly; 186-187: T. Kelly.

Note
The captioning of all the illustrations in this book has been the responsibility of Salamander Books Ltd and not of the individual contributors.